LIFE IN LYRICS

Channeling a Musician by Writing with Spirit Guides

Katie Lindler

Balboa Press books may be ordered through booksellers or by contacting:

Balboa Press
A Division of Hay House
1663 Liberty Drive
Bloomington, IN 47403
www.balboapress.com
844-682-1282

Illustrations:
Adobe Stock
Shutterstock

ISBN: 979-8-7652-4202-5 (sc)
ISBN: 979-8-7652-4201-8 (e)

Library of Congress Control Number: 2023908507

Print information available on the last page.

Balboa Press rev. date: 09/05/2023

www.katielindler.com
www.lifeinlyrics.com

For my husband, Lee

When I came out of the spiritual closet and told him I was channeling a musician and writing a book with Spirit Guides, he supported and believed in me.

Table of Contents

LIFE IN LYRICS

Channeling a Musician by Writing with Spirit Guides

Introduction

During a series of guided meditations, I discovered that a musician who wishes to be called Musique, is one of my Spirit Guides. He channels song lyrics and messages from the other side through Automatic Writing. This book is a compilation of the Automatic Writing or Channeled Writing I channeled with Musique and Spirit Guides. During this Automatic Writing process with Musique, other Spirit Guides, Archangels, and even ancestor spirits (my Grandpa Charlie) came through in between the song lyrics. Many of us refer to "the other side" as heaven, the afterworld, or behind the veil, eternal life, higher frequencies, or other dimensions, such as the fifth dimension and seventh dimension where there is unimaginable radiant light and unconditional love. This book provides a passage to higher frequency realms. The lyrical messages provide insight into life without fear and a new, higher energy vibration, the Love Vibration coming to Earth. When we tap into the energy of soul-connected intimacy, gratitude, and believing in limitless love and abundance, we discover the ability to expand our lives.

How did I connect with Musique on the other side?

During a virtual class called Esoteric Adventures by Michelle Gallagher, I met my Spirit Guide, Musique. Esoteric Adventures was a six-week online series where I learned how to enhance my intuition, telepathy, meditation, different types of divination, and was introduced to Spirit Guides and Archangels. During this class, my goal was to learn about my Spirit Guides and how to connect, communicate, and work with them. My second goal was to discover my personal divination methods. Channeling through Automatic Writing was indeed my special sauce of communication not just communicating with the other realms but as part of my life purpose. It was no surprise, more a validation really, because I have always felt a deep calling to write.
One night while working on my class assignment to connect and meet my Spirit Guides, the meditation guided through beautiful visuals of walking through a forest, down a path, breathtaking vistas, and light all around, leading to a bench. At the bench, I met my Spirit Guides.

Musique walked out of the veil of light and down the path from the opposite direction! He was dressed in a white suit and shirt, his hair and face looked like it did in his earlier days in his most recent life on Earth. His suit and fancy shirt, tailored, elegant, were accented with crystals.

Then, the guided meditation said my Spirit Guide would present me with a gift. Musique smiled and reached out and gave me a white box with rain inside it, drops shimmering with a violet flame. The meditation ended.

I listened to this meditation about ten times over the course of several weeks. To my surprise, Musique showed up again and again handing me gifts. Two times he gave me doves. Another time, he presented a music box shaped like a piano made out of clear glass with purple and turquoise accents.

When Musique walked away at the end of the session, a little boy would stand close and disappear with him down the path into the bright, white light of the veil. The little boy looked two or three years old with a precious smile, black curly hair with big, loose curls, and wearing a blue toddler's suit of shorts and collared jacket.

Though I had received doves, violet drops glowing like a purple flame in a box, a book with doves flying out of it, and a music box, I still wasn't sure what my new Spirit Guide Musique's messages were with all these gifts. I realized it had to do with music, but I didn't understand the full message. I talked with Michelle from the Esoteric Adventures class who suggested to Automatic Write about it, invite Musique to work with me through my Channeled Writing, ask for the answers, so I could understand his gifts and messages. That's how the Channeled Writing with Musique began. Song lyrics flowed down the page—one after another. Then, messages and stories came in lyrical form.

In this book, you will read these channeling sessions and discover the lyrics and messages that are meant for you. The messages from Spirit and Archangels that flowed are also included alongside Musique's words. The same cadence of the Channeled Writing sessions has been formatted in the book with Musique and the other Spirit Guides taking turns in a lyrical dance. Back and forth this channeling rhythm between them carried all the way through with:

- Musique's stories about life, love, music, trusting the flow, and expansion
- Song lyrics about relationships, sexy love, pain, music, a great awakening, Golden Age
- Spirit Guide insights and learning about the channeling process
- Trusting Spirit Guides

Since my Channeled Writing began, virtually every time I got in the car, one of Musique's songs played on the radio. Sometimes I asked my Spirit Guides to play another song if Musique my Spirit Guide was really there because, let's face it, your mind—your ego—doesn't want to believe it. To my amazement another song came on the radio on a different channel. One time, I was driving home from the airport after a business trip. I had done some Channeled Writing of song lyrics on the plane—the lyrics flowed through me. When I drove out of the airport and turned on the radio, three songs played on the radio from Musique. I laughed and cried, turned it up, and rocked out in astonishment most of the way home. This continued to happen.

While in the process of formatting and putting together this book, I was driving in my car, which didn't happen very often because of the stay-at-home orders during the COVID-19 pandemic. As the book was nearing completion, I wondered if Musique's songs would eventually stop. So, I asked for a song. After letting it go and not thinking about it, I changed the radio channel and there was one of his songs playing.

That is how I discovered the Spirit Guide Musique is with us. After we pass on, our souls live forever and still have missions to complete and co-create with us. Our souls continue to elevate. I learned that loving, high vibrational spirits and light beings are with us, too. They are guiding each one of us all the time and trying to send us messages and signs to communicate. Have you ever seen a cardinal or bluebird after someone you love passed away? It feels like it's there to tell you something. Have you ever felt your loved one who passed away was there with you? Ever see a bright sparkle of light in the room? Ever experience an unbelievable synchronicity where the timing of something or someone in your life appeared magically? Ever hear a song or see a billboard that gives you an a-ha moment with a solution, answer, or idea?

Ten years ago, I would have thought this was bullshit. Spirit Guides? You're out of your mind. In 2012, my heart opened to something I knew was always there. It felt like an awareness inside my soul woke up. The sudden death of my mother-in-law opened my consciousness to the light and help from Spirit Guides. The night she died, I felt a bone-chilling truth in my soul that she had been murdered. I was guided to evidence, as were my husband and sister-in-law. Over the grueling six years that followed, we fought the darkness her murderer cast around us. During this time, I embarked on a path to elevate my spirit and embrace my spiritual gifts. I followed the signs and synchronicities as I was guided to spiritual teachers, healers, shamans, and lightworkers who continue to teach me how to shine my light, step into my soul's purpose, and tap into Divine guidance.

As I continued my quest to enhance and develop my intuitive abilities, understand energy, frequency, and vibration, as well as use the power of gratitude and Law of Attraction to shape my life, people showed up who were experiencing similar spiritual awakenings. They felt the presence of their Spirit Guides and were heightening their senses, experiencing heightened extrasensory abilities in being able to see and feel energy with clairsentience, clairaudience, telepathy, and other techniques. We often refer to these types of people as empaths or empathic, intuitive, psychic, mediums, metaphysicians, and channelers. They are regular people, children, family members (often considered the odd ball, sensitive, or introverted one) friends, and business colleagues, as well as musicians, artists, and leaders. More people than we realize live their lives tapping into the vast power of universal love and energetic frequencies that are here for each one of us. When we are open to it—believe, feel good, and receive the messages waiting for us. Human beings have more powerful abilities than we know. In *Life in Lyrics* you will learn techniques on how to expand into your high vibrational power to build your life purpose.

When the Channeled Writing with Musique and my Spiritual Team began, our mission to help others expand became clear and failure wasn't an option. Finally, what I was doing was of service to others, by helping with their personal expansion. For the first time in my life, I was free of anxiety and stress in my work. I was creating what I was sent here to do.

Through guidance that came through the Automatic Writing and channeling Musique and other guides, I learned the goal was to publish this work and share it with the world at exactly the divine time that coincided with events and disclosures being revealed across the entire Earth. An awakening was occurring in people throughout the world. It was time to stand up and fight for LOVE to win, to save and protect the children, and our God-given freedoms.

Leading up to the publishing of *Life in Lyrics,* I would be guided to online resources where people from all walks of life, whether spiritual leaders, independent media, and regular people all experienced the same visions of awakened souls, finding the same information on mass spiritual awakening, and knowing deep in our souls something big beyond our imagination would soon happen on Earth to return us to the world we've always been meant to live in. If you've seen the movie, *Close Encounters of the Third Kind*, it's kind of like finally meeting other people that know exactly what's going on, as you do, but without the crazy antics. Or, like a scene in the book, *The Celestine Prophecy,* when you learn your true power and experience what life is like when you are in a higher vibration and frequency.

Awakening to our true human abilities such as co-creating our real life purpose through spiritual communication to other frequencies, and using the power of energy, vibration, and frequency to mold the life of our dreams remains the goal. Nothing would stop this from happening, and my Spiritual Team had me waiting backstage, so to speak, until it was the Divine's time for me to step into the beginning of the Golden Age serving as a bridge connecting people to the other side.

My purpose and the purpose of this book is to guide you to return to your true power and personal expansion. What better way to connect your mind and soul to your abilities and experience what being in the flow feels like than through the rhyming lyrics of music, a musician's stories, and how to connect with Spirit Guides.

There are millions of things that are real that we cannot see, hear, or touch, but we know they exist—viruses, the energy surrounding people, particles floating in the air, and God. We know it. We feel it. We believe it. Spirit Guides are more powerful than any virus or low energy surrounding you. If you believe in the effects of a virus, wait until you see the positive experiences that show up when you connect and work with your Spiritual Team. Expect solutions. Expect more love. Expect miracles. Expect healing.

How to Work with this Book

There are a lot of creative ways to work with this book. You'll find your own way. One way is to read the book as you would any novel or nonfiction book, straight through from beginning to end. The song lyrics and messages from Spirit Guides, The Divine, and Archangels are organized by chapters with themes. From the musician's stories to the song lyrics, and techniques on channeling through writing with Spirit Guides, you will experience an energy shift, a higher vibration, a trip to the other side, and receive answers to how life is meant to be for each one of us. There is life all around us that we can't see with our eyes, but we can learn how to see it. All our souls (our light, our spirit) are connected whether here on Earth or in the "afterlife" on the other side, and throughout the galaxies.

Another way you may work with this material is like an oracle and divination textbook and enjoy jumping around the book to read different sections. Here's how it works. Before you open the book, ask your Spiritual Team that's of the highest vibration of pure light to show you what you need to know at this time. Feel good, trust, and open to a page without thinking. The page you open to is the message or sign you are meant to receive at that time. Close your eyes while opening to a page, if that feels good to you. Don't over think it. In fact, don't think at all. The page the book opens to and where your eyes are drawn on the page is where you are being guided. Perhaps there are song lyrics meant for you, a message about something you've gone through in one of the musician's stories, answers about the awakening you're experiencing in your life, and what's happening on Earth and in the universe.

About The Lyrical Writing Styles

Many things fascinate me about the words I channeled in this book. There is something big happening within the lyrics. One of the channeled messages I received: certain people are meant to discover this book and experience the magic power in the music and lyrics. The book will find those it is meant for, elevate their lives, and help heal the energy of the world that benefits all of us.

Another point of fascination with the words I was channeling is two different styles of writing arrived through the Channeled Writing sessions. The first style was song lyrics. Lyrics came through with verse and chorus and some even with notes about the instruments. It was crystal clear those communications were songs. I was strictly guided to present how the lyrical flow came through in the songs being channeled, to not change or perfect the format nor add anything to the songs.

With the lyrics as a common theme throughout and the channeling coming from a musician, the book is organized in the format of Set One, Set Two, and Encore, just as a band organizes their playlist at a live concert. Enjoy the rhythm elevating and the show.

The second style of channeling through Automatic Writing, including from Musique, were words filling a page without a break in a paragraph or sentence. I typed or hand wrote words nonstop down full 8 inch by 11 inch pages at astonishing speed. It was effortless! I had no hesitation. I could feel the presence of my Spirit Guides working through me, as we co-created. Of course, every now and then, my mind and ego said, *holy smokes look at this*, but I learned to quiet my mind and return to the flow.

It wasn't until I went back to read the Channeled Writing that the rhyming lyrics jumped out at me and sent a shockwave through my heart. Often, I wrote late at night after a long workday. By the time the writing stopped for the night, I was so tired. Immediately, I went to sleep and read the writing the next day or so. I don't remember everything I wrote with my Spirit Guides. It was an amazing experience to go back and read what was channeled. I thought, it can't be! These are all lyrics! Rhyming lyrics! Going through the pages and pages of my Channeled Writing sessions to discover the flow of rhyming lyrics through a musician's story, discover instructions on how to achieve communication with Spirit Guides, how to live in a higher frequency, and that we will soon be experiencing a Golden Age of abundance and energy expansion was one of the most profound experiences I have ever had.

Of note on the multiple poetic rhythms, it wasn't until I was in the editing and formatting phase of publishing, when I noticed the numerous poetic rhythms within the channeled lyrics. There are various lengths of meter in the channeling including internal rhymes, end rhymes, couplets, as well as triple and quadruple lines rhyming. It hadn't crossed my mind that there could be some poetic structure within the lyrics other than free verse in this Channeled Writing.

It is an extraordinary feeling of faith and honor to be of service and co-create a book of rhyming lyrics with Spirit Guides, and to share with you how to do it. Spirit Guides are available to anyone who will open to them and practice. From behind the veil, Spirit Guides of the highest vibration of healing surround you with unconditional love. Only love exists and their guidance is always available to you.

What is Channeled Writing or Automatic Writing with Spirit Guides?

Channeled Writing or Automatic Writing is channeling a Spirit Guide from the spiritual realm through writing. Automatic Writing is the process of receiving messages from guides on the other side and letting the words flow freely upon the page as you type or handwrite on paper. Your body and mind are in a clear, positive, and meditative state. Channeled Writing or Automatic Writing is letting words flow freely upon the page without judgment, editing, or hesitation. The process comes from your soul, connecting to the universal light of your Spirit Guides. It is an opportunity to connect your light to the realms above and beyond. It's a trip to another dimension and higher frequencies. In Channeled Writing, you don't think about what you write, which is a technique that can be learned.

At the end of the book, you will find a chapter on my Channeled Writing process and insight channeled through angels and guides on how the technique works and how to start using the technique for yourself. Even if you're not interested in learning the process, you will discover more answers from Archangels and benevolent Light Beings to elevate your life, as you continue to shift into a higher vibration.

The Writing Process with Musique the Spirit Guide

In full disclosure and transparency of the process, I never looked up anything about Musique's past lives or work before the Channeling and Automatic Writing began. I was instructed by my Spiritual Team through the channeling to trust the Automatic Writing process and not let my ego-mind try to control the process by researching, which would ultimately destroy the whole mission of learning to be 100% in the flow with Spirit Guides. This came easy to me, because I've never had an interest in following lives of many popular people. I enjoy artists' work but people's personal lives have never interested me to go out of my way to follow.

During the process, I looked up a few names that came through, because I thought the Channeled Writing had misspellings or typos, like My Love's name, for example, who Musique refers to as his twin flame in the channeling in this book. I had never heard the name before. Names and descriptive words from the original Channeled Writing were changed to respect personal identity laws.

There are lyrics in my channeling with Musique and other Spirit Guides that came through about people's lives. The guidance I received from my Spirit Guides throughout channeling these lyrical words is that the words, song lyrics, and messages have meaning and purpose for God, the Akashic Record, and to people who are meant to find them. The stories channeled by Musique have meaning to the healing and personal expansion of many people. I am presenting what I channeled in the lyrical stories from Musique without providing any analysis, context, or meaning. That's not my purpose, nor the purpose of this book. The purpose of the book including the musician's stories is for the reader to experience and learn what it feels like to trust being in the flow. What better way to experience the flow and co-creating with Spirit Guides than with a musician. If any lyrics find their way to your heart and soul, they are meant to ignite a spark of love and awakening to help you expand in your life.

If I hadn't done what was asked of me by my Spirit Guides, which was to share these lyrics and lesson from working with a Spiritual Team, my soul would have failed one of its biggest assignments. Why me? Why am I the channel? The answers are in the lyrics.

So here it is. For you. The Spirit Guides have come through me, but ultimately they are here for you and all the world. I wouldn't be surprised if Musique may be guiding others in different ways. I hope you find what's meant for you within the musician's stories, song lyrics, and guide to learning about our expansion through Channeled Writing. Let's begin our journey with Spirit Guides.

SET ONE

Over The Rainbow We Go

Chapter 1
Learning About Musique and Being in the Flow

Chapter 2
A Musician's Life

Chapter 3
Trusting Spirit Guides Through Archangel Gabriel, The Divine, and Musique's Life

Chapter 1

Learning About Musique and Being in the Flow

It wasn't until I was putting the Channeled Writings together in the book that I realized I was being taught to learn and trust the guidance and flow with Spirit Guides just as much as the reader would be, perhaps for the first time. Beginning in Chapter 1, Musique the musician Spirit Guide and the Spiritual Team channel about the flow and process, then shift to share Musique's stories. This cadence of learning to be in the flow and learning about Musique's stories happened during the Automatic Writing process, so I wanted the reader to start out experiencing the same flow I did while channeling.

We begin to discover the purpose of the book, the energy of being in the flow, discovering Musique's stories, and step into the higher energy and vibration the Spirit Guides bring. You may feel calm and sleepy. You may get goosebumps or feel tingles. We are going over the rainbow and sliding down to the other side. Your soul knows how to get there, so your mind can confidently and quietly follow along side.

Learning about Musique and Being in the Flow

Here's where we begin to feel the cadence of the story in the lyrics.
Your invitation into the light with Great Spirit.
This book is about faith, trust, and feeling in the flow,
Learning to let your mind go,
Releasing your thoughts on wanting to figure out and know
who I was. The purpose of this book is for you to connect with your soul,
Let your higher-self lead,
Ask your ego to step away, so you can be connecting on a higher frequency.
You may start to feel fuzzy headed or sleepy,
You may get goosebumps or see a sparkle of light,
As you read, you will be transported to the other side,
When your mind quiets its need to analyze.
There is a message for you,
Whether you read the book all the way through,
Or jump around and pick different parts to read, or both, however you choose,
Ask your Spirit Guides of the highest vibes,
To show you messages and lyrics inside,
Meant for your soul to find.
In the book, you will hear this several times,
Turn off your mind.
Life in the flow is led by your soul. Ready to go?
Follow us over the rainbow,
Oh yes, there is gold.

Give Faith a Look in the Purpose of This Book

The purpose of this book is to show,
You are so much more than you know.
You are not just a physical body with a big ego and mind,
You are connected to the unseen spiritual realm all the time.
You have a soul, a light inside you, that yearns to work with your Spirit Guides,
If you've been guided to this book, your Guides are saying, *we're here by your side.*

You are so much more,
Than this one current life you may find hard or adore,
You have had other lives before.
Like me, you are not just one person,
Who you are right now includes your past life lessons.
Why do you struggle with recurring troubles and you can't figure out why?
Many struggles we choose are patterns to conquer from past lives.
Your life here is not just about you,
You chose to come back to elevate more, so what are you going to do?

Music is so much more than you may know,
When songs and lyrics are channeled and created from your soul,
Your ego can step to the side and let the co-creation flow,
When the lyrics, musical production and every instruments notes,
Are co-created with your Spiritual Team,
Whether aware of it or not, the divine flow elevates the world and your dreams.

Writing is so much more than you know,
The energy that fills pages and songs, when writing with your guides in the flow,
Comes from the spiritual realm on high vibe frequencies,
When you work with your Spiritual Team,
To create the writing or anything meant for your life purpose to succeed,
You are answering your soul's calling and your own soul contract decisions,
As well as a divine plan that includes your Spirit Guides' missions.
We are each co-creating; you are not alone,
I am The Artist, Musique, and though I have been well known,
In past lives, my missions include other shows,
Like here with you now as a Spirit Guide, to help you awaken to your power,
We'll show you how we do this through lyrics and you will discover,
You can learn to connect with your Spiritual Team, too,
We love you and we are always right here for you.
Like an amp switch, flick on our connection by asking for help, and be ready to groove.
See how we do this effortlessly?
With faith, asking for help, and releasing any negativity,
Prepare to expand your mind and soul through lyrics with me.
Expansion is the new Age of Energy, the Golden Age is your destiny,
You shall see.

Rise of The Artist, Musique

The show is my heaven, it is where God makes me, me,
I leave it all behind and for everyone to see,
This is me, this is Musique, this is how I rock and shake my core,
This is how I go down in history, this is how much I want this more,
I want this more than anything, I need the show to feel alive,
Be myself on stage and leave it behind,
When I connect to Spirit, I didn't know it, but I get taken over,
By the flow, the co-creators,
It comes through me and my guitar.
Is beauty something you reflect on and decide hey that's really gorg,
Or do you find it when you're rocking,
When the exchange and peddle lock the floor?
The music swirls through the air and in a moment you feel like never before.
What happened? You elevated off the stage, outer body,
Music brings you back down like a floating dove.
You leave your body, and Spirit anchors you there,
As you escape and mingle with the sound,
Waves and energy expanding all around,
See the music like colors and rainbows of chords, and notes as far as the eye can see,
We see it flying all over you, in the distance we hear the band going on and fans scream,
Up and down the aisle as we make the music last,
For a long while and into the darkness,
With the one bright spotlight on your face,
Feels hot and sometimes daunting, until you know just what this makes.
It makes you a superstar,
Not for the people, but for your power,
Superpower to ignite the souls of others, who need love more and more,
You can give love and know,
It is coming back to you ten-fold,

I see it all around and wonder why can't I have more, but I realize I do,
I have love and I know how to give it, too.
Look at all these people grooving and being part of me,
I will get it funky,
I get it excited. I love to make the beauties feel,
More beautiful than before,
Leave them with a song that touches hearts, so they can do more,
More for their people, for their loved ones,
For the others that couldn't come,
Don't have fans to help them.
If your music could touch someone,
Make a difference, do it all over just for them,
For that one person to give them inspiration,
They have what it takes to make it,
To be the one on the other side, like this,
Helping more love come through,
On this journey that elevates them and more people to do,
The same thing, to expand and believe in this new life,
New beginnings, a time of better times,
When more people open up to a greater love,
A greater love for everyone, for all things, it is time to rise above,
Let the music flow,
Let the hearts go, let the sound flow,
Let the ideas go,
Go out on papers and not stash them away to forget and say no.
Don't inspire others to do a silly thing or nothing at all,
Life is expecting you to flourish. You can do it all. Be the one you are meant to be,
Let's do this for everyone and see them smiling and realizing,
How inviting and meant to be it is,
You have what it takes,
To share who you are and instantly feel an escape,
Into a full life for all of you to shine through,

If you hear me know that I am saying, I love you.
I want more for you and all that is,
You can have what you want. You have what it takes,
Be the one who knows he or she can do it.
I've never seen anyone as fast as you,
The powers you have to bring it through,
Quite fascinating to see our light connected, impacting a page,
Impacting a world, a new loving world for all to see,
When they see, it will be a spark, a match flash, like holy smokes what did I just see and feel?
Ain't no fooling around, this is the real deal.

Now shake it,
You can't go on like this,
Not shaking it enough,
You gotta shake that thing and do that somethin' only your sugar's got.
Now get all sexy and rise above
that fear and grab a hold of the dove.
The dove that flies in and brings shimmering drops of violet waves to shine your shoes,
Your shoes sparkle like the ocean as the sun glistens,
On a bright day you say to yourself,
"I am a sparkling diamond in the rough,"
I got what it takes now let me get it would ya, I got more where this came from,
I feel it instantly and I know,
You are there to guide me, I feel it in my guitars and bones,
I know I can make music with you.

I feel a diamond light in the sky and seven as they surround,
I believe in rainbows, I followed one down,
Here through the veil,
On this page, let the rhythm steer the wheel.
A wheel of consciousness and of dreaming of being in the flow with you,
All the people, I see you. I know what you can do!

I had a fascinating experience,
Bringing my joy to everyone who would listen,
To their own hearts, I had a vision,
Dedicate my vision to them,
A vision to have forever, then dedicate it when they're dead,
To let the legacy live on forever and dedicate it some more,
Be the peace and the wonder and excitement forever.

It can be a mystery to unfold all the secrets,
I can bring to the table more specifics.
Life went so fast, I never slowed down. I hibernated, but I couldn't sleep,
I was awake forever, my spirit was amped, not quite complete.
It didn't matter that My Love was with someone else and I alone,
I had this business, all this acreage, and what was I to do,
I keep on playing and play on,
Because that was how you follow through on being bold,
Being free, and let's face it, escaping from the cold.
Those cold-ass winters, they were brutal in my city, to the core they'd get you, chill those bones,
Grey the skies and damn get me out of here, I would say,
A longing always brought me back to where I always said I'd stay.
An experience I never in a million years thought I knew,
Something about her, that girl so fine, it was something I had to prove.
She had a blue coat on and diamond rings, big ones in her ears,
A tape recorder in her hands to tell me she'd make me a star,
She had me pegged to be the one badass, a master with his guitar.
It was more about the music than anything,
I had a passion,
A flame, I could never put it out,
It was a massive bonfire that crackled up to the heavens and never went out,
Until one day when I fell on my face,
Met my maker and wrote down my vision, when I became awake.
I saw something when I crashed so hard. I knew I had a message to bring through,

It inspired me to write music for others. See what they could do,
With the songs I wrote that came from my guardian angels, now I know,
They worked through me,
Nudged me to give songs away,
To the right person they always went,
Damn those songs, my babies, they grew, they were heaven sent.
Artists that give their passion to others,
Well, some are guided to do it more,
I felt an urgency in my need to, and thought, oh hell, this is perfect for you,
See what you can do.
Bam! The magic followed them right through the track,
Once they dropped, I would sit back,
Like a proud daddy, celebrate the birth,
What you can do for others,
Well, nothing compares to what you get from that self-worth.
I'd give all the songs away in my notebooks,
I feel their rhythms. I remember how much time I took,
I know who they are for,
I didn't know at the time, but now I see, it is clear,
If I can reach them from here,
They will find their person that is for sure.
There's nothing your mind has to try to know, when you're living in the flow.

In the Flow With Musique
Letting Go of Mind Control

When was the last time you went with the flow,
Cleared your mind of judgment and needing to control,
Every little thought and thing in your life,
Like thinking you knew me or My Love, my soulmate wife?
We've tried for nearly two years to get ahold of My Love,
We have sent writings only she would know and even doves.
It was a lesson in faith and in trusting yourself and your Spirit Guides,
Katie waited patiently, continued Channeled Writing and grew more wise.
While we were waiting, she followed her guides,
Then, dropping seemingly out of the sky, she realized,
Like, shazam! A massive download from us to her, bridging our sides,
The message was clear, the Divine had spoken,
She had suddenly woken and our clear path was chosen.
Having patience with Divine timing and believing,
The time for the book is here, and expansion is what you will all be receiving.
If you are reading this, the book is for you,
Turn off your ego-mind, so your soul connects through.
The veil thins,
Messages for you come in to sink in,
Let's begin.

I am not who you thought I am. I am so much more. I was a star,
Yes true, but I am so much more than one life I had, just like you are.
The point of intentionally leaving out past lives names,
Is so your mind will let go of trying to make claims,
Thinking you knew me, because you were a big fan,
Why does this channeler think she can?

Who in the world is she to be a channeler for me?
Well, it wasn't her idea, that's the point, don't you see?
If Katie hadn't had faith, trusted her Spirit Guides and gone with Divine flow,
You wouldn't be reading these lyrics, your soul would never go,
Where we are taking you, because it's never been done like this before.

When you follow your calling, it's like answering God's call,
No one ever said it wouldn't feel scary, no, not at all,
But that feeling of fear is an illusion created by your mind.
Your soul and Spirit Guides,
Help make your vision, your purpose, come true,
You each have a team of spirit experts always with you,
If you aren't seeing their signs or seeing them but not following through,
Your mind is too controlling, time to give it a rest,
With your soul leading, you will always see success,
Maybe not in the form you think, that's the fun part, so never second guess.

St. Germain Explains Past Lives and Spirit Guides

I have been many people in past lives, like a father and an artist like Musique,
My original soul essence,
Carries the violet flame,
Some people know as St Germain,
In one life I sang,
Wrote songs about the beauty of women, the Divine Feminine, and rainy days,
To expand transformation through the violet rays,
As light, which we all come from,
We are all made of,
Let your soul sink into knowing you have known this before,
You are waking up, as is every person on Earth,
Your amazing life has just started, it's like you've just been birthed,
Because the old ways of the world have crumbled,
Giving way to a new you that is humbled,
Honored and blown away,
To be experiencing history never created this way.
Legions of angels, galactic star people, ancestors, and light beings,
Work as I do as Spirit Guides, helping you expand and to see,
This is real and your Spiritual Team is prepared,
To guide you to work with them, they are full of love and care.
They may be family or other spirits with past connections to your soul's work,
You are here to co-create; expanding love always remains first,
On our list of work to do,
Nothing can stop your light from what you're meant to do,
Except for you and your free will,
So, focus on how much you know your true self,
You each have a mission; your Spirit Guides are here to help.

The point of all this rhyming is so your mind quiets,
For your soul to continue climbing,
To experience a particular rhythm of being in the flow,
Learning how to let go,
To trust and feel the flow, have faith in what your Spirit Guides know,
For you to expand your light,
Grow massive love in your life.
What a time to be alive.
When you feel lost open your heart and close your mind,
For in your heart you will hear our voice and your soul you will find.

Where the Essence of Spirit Lies

It is in the beauty that surrounds us,
In the spirit realm, it's magnetic like a lighting source,
Turn on your love light and in an instant illuminate your course.
There is more of the story to unfold,
There is much that Great Spirit has in store,
For you and Mary, Joseph's Mary, that gave birth to the king,
He's watching over you and has another story to begin.
You're the one to tell it, we'll write it through you for all to find,
Butterflies and zebras talk and dogs know, they can read your mind,
So can the daisies and the flowers and the trees,
They all feel the energy you give off,
Believe in positive thinking, it's a bottle rocket that can launch
you into the stars or down to hell, so watch your vibe and bring it high,
In the sky not far from Jupiter, there's another civilization flying by.
They're peaceful and advanced, and they know how to make time fly
much faster than you,
On Earth it's slower on purpose, so you feel and think your way through,
Back to the place that you came from in the heavens,
Where we all stay one day.
Spirit brings us passion and our freedom that we seek,
You'll find it in your purpose, there's no one to compete,
With your Divine power, it's in the words that you create,
With Spirit, the angels and me, and your Grandpa Charlie, that's our fate.
Get ready, for the engine is revved up and it's going full throttle,
You always wanted to go fast, so better give us a holler,
This time fast seems like the perfect pace,
When you're doing what you want, there's not a minute to waste.
Be open and ready and prepared to make a change into the person you've wanted to become,
You've always been that person, but now it's turned on.

Now go to bed and get some rest.
You're getting better at channeling us.
Be open to what happens, don't over think it at all.
I see you soaring, we all do, so just let it happen, be yourself and let it flow.
Flow's a word we call the magic, the Divine connection and awe of you,
Spirit has the answers and channels them through writers like you,
So stay steady, give it time but not much longer and you'll be, well, you'll see.
Watch your thoughts; stay positive-va,
That's where the magic happens, in the positive vibes-za!
We love ya.

Why Musique is Here

To make things clear,
I felt alone in this world; I took a step away,
There's a time in your life when you feel the pain is going to stay.
You look into your eyes in the mirror, you see scared,
What's looking back at you isn't pretty, it's not you, there's someone else there.
You take a little more, you don't mean to, that's how it goes,
The next thing you know you're on the floor after the dose.
I didn't mean it. It wasn't fate that brought me there.
There's another thing I need and that's to give this song to Great Spirit now,
A crowd pleaser for tomorrow, an iconic award, take a bow.

Do yourself a favor give it up to those you love,
They need your spirit in their aura, make them feel good and float like a dove,
Like the doves in the box I gave you, so white, and they didn't make a sigh,
In heaven there's no crying, but the rain, it's a violet flame in our sky,
It's the colors of the rainbow and you can slide down just for fun,
The children laugh and sing here, no one is left with anyone.
We all share our lives and dreams together,
Make this world a magic place,
You'll see it when you get here, dreams are real, there is no race.
Feel the magic in your heart. Shake the fear out of your mind,
Watch the booze, drugs, bad men, and girls that always whine.
It isn't easy in your life but it's not meant to be so hard, you see,
For if I could do it over, I'd be rockin' on my knees,
An angel you always hoped for by your side, always in your hour of need,
He's with me and we drop by to see My Love in her garden while she feeds,
A special statue with the birdseed in the back by the hedge so long,
I'll tell her in a love song that we love her, even though I'm gone,
She is a miracle for this world; she keeps her strength and carries on.

To see her in that robe again it's pink and flows like wine,
It's smooth and silky to the touch. She's an angel that was all mine,
Tell her that I love her, I'm watching over her daily grind.
We are with her. It is Musique and her angel that loves her so dear,
I am with her always, in the night I hear her pour those tears,
The light surrounds her now and she can let go and be free,
There's a miracle awaiting just for her and soon she will see.

The music when I play it in heaven the angels sing,
For you and me and the baby spirits,
They are free, and love is what they bring,
Every hour of the day until you are with us again,
So wait for that miracle, it is always on time, you will see,
If I could do it over, it would mean I'd even sing for free.
In freedom there is wealth and without money we'd still make it to the top,
When you elevate your energy, that is when you can never stop,
Believing in yourself and all that magic it's freakin' real.

Losing My Love and Playin' On

I'm flying to the next gig, you all take the bus,
Deliver me to the hotel room and don't make a fuss.
I was getting a little too big for my britches,
My tight ass delivered on divine wishes,
I was in the flow so much the vibrations were magnetic,
I pulled so many toward me, felt good to know they got it.
A phone in the sound booth rang in the middle of the night,
I wasn't quite surprised,
Nonetheless jumped with fright,
How was I supposed to know she'd be leaving me,
I was hoping she'd dance all night,
In the night of my soul, and in my day delight.
I slept in the afternoon, thought about her and that time in the rain,
I wasn't too used to sleeping without my sweet thing,
I missed her and longed for her deeply, but my music kept me going,
When I saw my eyes in the mirror, and thought what are you doing?
I played on and kept my life steady,
God, I missed her but would never say,
When two loves separate that shouldn't, it is like an earthquake,
In your heart and in the galaxies, we'll be together again someday.
What if I could do it over and bring her back some joy in life?
When one heart expands, so do all the rest, it's one reason you are all alive,
Together at the same time, you all planned to be here at exactly the same time,
I left my rhythm behind me once, and I'm coming back to get her with the Divine.

She has that force to shine, that angel that was all mine,
Brighter than the star of Bethlehem, sharper than a tack on a stair,
Don't go easy on her, let her know how much you care,
No sugar coating the pain, it was real and it hurt so bad,
At the time life was hard, but I keep the good times we had,
Brings in that inner light, when I remember how many lives I've been a dad.

There's an angel with me, I see him now,
He never leaves your side, even when you take a bow,
Are you thinking, *but I want to know how*?
Oh you know, your intuition and spirit always knows,
How to connect with the other side and where he goes,
You watch over his heart and he watches over you,
Watch for the signs, the signs of I love you,
Be at peace, know your worth,
Follow your dreams through on this Earth,
We will guide you to an ever better life of your dreams,
The path may appear wild or new or so it would seem,
The artist in you, that producer wants to create,
More and more around you will continue to elevate.
You are guided here by your own divine knowing,
Trusting what is next for you is when the magic starts flowing,
I'll give you the sign and you will know it is me, your Musique,
Now then, you ready? Great, let's do this.

Now Let's Do This As I Wish

Set my songs in my notebooks free,
Give them away to artists with no fee,
After the music's made the powers that be receive a royalty,
Fans continue to share in the magic that is my legacy,
A place of solitude for romantic walks and dreamers to see how following their wish helps others grow,
My dream still remains to share with the people everything I know,
Your true essence continues to expand after you slide down the rainbow,
Share a song with a loving soul,
Whose mission is to make it fly,
Fly through the ethers, heard through the galaxies and never have to say goodbye,
Because I am here, the spiritual revolutionaries understand why.

I talked about it in music sessions about the afterworld, when we pass on,
Unbeknownst to me at the time,
Though we hoped together that we didn't have to say goodbye,
We promised we would find each other,
When one of us went to the other side,
So, here I am as a Spirit Guide,
Continuing my mission to connect with you,
You see, there is no end, this is one of my next beginnings with more to do.
My hope is you publish this work without my name there, because my true loved ones will know,
I love you more than green grass on an ocean floor with mermaids tickling my toes,
My light and soul continue on forever, and my mission right now is this show.
I play through lyrics from this side,
Give my love and birth of a new song meant for the music makers to find,
When they do, get ready, because there is no stopping an artist's magnetic force to shine.

Their massive bright light can bring a groove to all of you,
Get ready because when music is made you will experience a higher vibe,
Higher than you ever thought possible, now let's do this, let's feel alive.
Feel joy, feel ecstasy,
Laughing so hard your tears flow and you dance,
I am always here for you, this is Musique.
Now, let's do this.

You got it, go shine,
Deliver the goods and you will find,
I meant this for you all along,
It didn't take much for you to bring through our songs.
Know this is here for you to elevate the earth,
Bring together people to share in this work.
I delivered the goods, now you deliver your love,
Continue to spread the rise of the dove.
Into the music, I always reside,
Know in my soul you were there for me this time, for me to find,
To continue our mission, our goal to light up the world with this vision,
Do the good the Divine's requested of us, for our life purpose and mission,
Give them hope, give them inspiration,
Be love people can share and expand the celebration,
The world is about to get amazing with star people on the horizon,
The magic power of life in lyrics is just the beginning of new manifestation,
Power will be amplified for all on the planet, no more division.
You each will manifest what you want and dream of even faster,
So think of the positive not thoughts of disaster,
Your thoughts are the reality that makes your life around you,
Believe and feel good, think of what you want to do.
I won't go away, I am here as the Divine needs me to be,
With all the love in the world, our spirits are free,
There is so much more love and light than the dark stuff than you can imagine,

Be in the Light of God and you continue expansion.
Peace, My Love, peace to you all,
We are in this together, answer the call.
Ringing in your ears, that spark of excitement in your heart,
That's us trying to get through to you, watch for the signs we send, then start,
Begin a new way of thinking and doing, live your best life together, not apart.
You need one another and on the other side we need you,
The great awakening event brings our dimensions together soon,
Remember when you need help, ask us, and we will come through,
Now go, believe in yourselves, we love and believe in you.

When Musique Died, Went to the Other Side, Became a Guide

I think about you all the time,
An easy feeling on my mind,
Dreaming of the day when we sat on a bench,
Smiled at each other with wide eyes content.
Your light was much more beautiful than I had imagined,
I wanted to take you and show you what happened,
The day I died evidently it was a mistake on my fate; I went away too soon,
I followed the rainbow over the moon,
I was greeted by a boy, he was maybe about two,
He tugged at me and jumped in my arms,
By the fate he was given by God's holy hand,
I knew the moment I saw this angel boy that I was his Dad,
Meant to come back to heaven early so I could show him the way,
The way into eternal salvation where the angels play.
He took my hand to walk me over to the window to see you,
I gazed from the veil and thought could it be true,
I was meant to write music from the spirit world to give you,
You'd care for my music like a baby making sure my songs grew and grew,
Into what Spirit desires for all of us,
Make music to last forever,
Now you know what we have to do, it's a must.
Thinking of the rhythm and funky beats,
I'll take care of planting that in musicians, you take care of the word heat,
It will get hot and steamy with emotion,
You can bet when she reads it, her heart feels an explosion,
You'll ignite a fire in her soul, she'll want to kiss
you on the cheek and squeeze you tight, something I don't plan to miss.
Trust your instincts and feel your power in your divination as you write,
No one can do what you do, you're with me, feel the light.

CHAPTER 2

A Musician's Life

In between the automatic writing about Musique's stories and learning how to be in the flow with the Spirit Guides, song lyrics about music life from a musician's perspective came through me effortlessly. Most of the song lyrics were channeled late at night or during flights, when my energy was most open. I wrote down the time on most of my Automatic Writing because it always astounded me how fast the writing came through. Most of the song lyrics were channeled in 15 to 30 minutes. All the songs were channeled in under 45 minutes, from growing up with the passion to play, to life on the road, notes for band members, and Musique wanting us to learn how to connect with the other side. A musician's calling often continues on the other side, just in a higher frequency serving as a co-creator Spirit Guide.

From Chapter 2 through Chapter 6, the song lyrics I channeled did not come through with perfect songwriting composition, and I was guided that it is not my purpose to edit or add perfect structure to the lyrics. How these lyrics came through have significant meaning to Musique and to people meant to discover them, so I followed my Spirit Guides mission respectfully from my soul, rather than what my mind wanted to control. Each time a song came through in my channeling, it would start with verses, then a chorus, then the rest of the verses. Sometimes a bridge would appear or notes on the bridge or instrumental arrangement.

Beginning in Chapter 2 and through Chapter 6 is where the three prominent rhythms of channeling come together: song lyrics, Musique's stories for you to feel into the flow, and guidance on what connecting with Spirit Guides and/or the other side, "heaven," looks and feels like. Music is the language of our heart and soul, and what an ideal way to experience being in the flow with Spirit Guides.

Raising a Music Child

Shouldn't it be time for you to leave?
Take your brother with you, if you please.
Don't stop at the store on the way there,
Don't forget the milk. Look at you, I can't take you anywhere.
Think you gonna get some piece of ass dressed like that?
Well maybe nothing special but some broad that's been with too many cats.
It ain't easy being you but you don't have to be so damn scared all the time,
Those drums, guitar and singing, banging around and damn all those rhymes,
Just doodling never noodling, always going too fast, not working hard in school,
Son you better get some good grades this time, you remember the rule,
Practice after school after you do your homework,
Bed by 10pm and don't sneak back out your room for more dessert.
Winter is coming, these cold ass winters, when we wished we lived in Hollywood,
With the sun and the stars and damn I would get us there if I could.
Now go get yourself something to eat, and wash that guitar case, it's looking bad,
Fill your cup with something sweet and don't forget to talk to your Dad.
Sometimes I think you remind me of him, but then I see you look more like me,
Well, you have my face and my grace at least,
When you grow up we shall see,
Just who goes to college or music school,
Or becomes a star with all that band racket coming out of your room,
And what's the deal with me always hearing the sound and words you say, "sonic boom?"
I'm sick of hearing that now son, go find another tune,
A new one for us to hear over and over coming out of your room.

We know you get up in the middle of the night with those headphones on, music banging loud inside your ears,
Don't think I don't know what you're up to and have been all these years.
Now give your mama a kiss good night, before I start cleaning or sitting down to take a rest,
You know I love you now sugar, you have always been my best,
Who listened to me without getting too nasty and talking back and putting me to the test,
If you can do something great one day, I hope you get yourself out of this mess,
The mess of always having to fight so hard for what you want and giving your pay away to Uncle Sam,
When he ain't giving shit back to you, that's right, these crooked politicians don't give a damn.
So go on now and go do something spectacular and get yourself a star on the sunset strip,
You know I ain't joking, when I see my boy with that special gift,
The Lord has blessed you with an almighty power, make no mistake,
You have big plans to go and make it,
Now go play mama a new tune she can dance to one that's gonna be a number one hit.

Power in Music

When I was young I felt a pain inside my head,
Music was bursting through me in the darkness of my bed,
Bedtime was when I'd hear the words,
Feel the music roar through me, instead
of sleeping I'd put on my earphones and rock out on the floor,
When you're young your room can be a safe haven, the artist in you free to explore,
It's like you're not alone, the music is your best friend,
Guiding you through the end,
To the next beat that comes to your mind,
Like it has been there all the time,
Waiting for you to let go and discover what's in the rhyme,
I have the power in my music that God has meant for you to find.

[Chorus]
Get the power in music,
Get the power is music,
Get the power in music,
The power is music.

Don't sit quietly turn it up now,
Crank that amp and electric guitar,
Feel the bass and the keys and my percussionist drumming like a star,
One of my first songs was made in a day, and others took no time too,
Everyone can do it if you pull deep from inside of you,
Open your heart up, detach from control, and hear that voice,
The one that seems to come out of nowhere, that is when you make the choice,
To listen without judgment, follow the thought and bring it through,
The lyrics, the drums, and keyboard - that sound is meant for you.

Don't get weary when the idea isn't on time, so you think,
It's never going out of reach,
Listen to the instant thought, for in it there is something to teach,
Music makes miracles happen in this universe, the energy shakes our core,
Conquers evil in our hearts, and now our souls are restored,
To live on a higher vibe where angels and ancestors soar.
Oh oh oh. Oh oh oh. Oh oh oh oh.

Studio Flow

It was another day of when we were together,
I could see it in your eyes and felt light as a feather,
I went to the recording studio and played a song for me,
At that moment I remembered I was free,
To be who I wanted and to explore some more of me,
Inside I was dying, if I couldn't set my true reality.

[Chorus]
In the flow, find your rhythm,
In the flow, it's your grace,
In the flow, find your rhythm,
In the flow, it's heaven's embrace.

You make me nervous when I see you, it's something I can't explain,
I look through the studio doorway and it's you there again,
Waiting for me to give myself to you,
I feel shy like the person I don't want to be,
I thought that was the real me,
Acting mysterious and uncomfortably.

So I took out a pen and paper and guitar,
Bought a six pack and some smokes and headed out the door,
To the only place that mattered,
Inside my head and with music,
For the flow to hit the paper and chords and rhythm to click,
It's like inhaling Jesus (I imagine), and it shakes your core,
Without faltering for a moment, I started jamming and feel it more,
Escaping to the beat, to the time, and to the bass,
It's a natural feeling, like the comfort of an embrace.

Don't give up on your music, everyone has their own rhythm to find,
You can sing it, you can build it, you can talk it and you can glide,
Through this world meant for you, find the beauty that's inside,
Get out of your own way, let others be right,
Your power is in not feeling enough to hurt others and start a fight.

Your music means nothing, unless it comes from love and grace,
Once you stop controlling, you elevate to a higher place,
Where the magic is, it floats high above the sky,
Not out of reach for the believers and the ones who hope to die,
Doing what they were meant for and let the world watch them pass by.

Blues in the Vault

Jump on a litter box screen in the sand,
Don't think about it, I'll give you a hand,
Despite all the things we've said, I don't give a damn,
Let's start over, forget about bad times, learn from our past.

Elegant blues can reveal a shadowy side to you,
I keep my bright light close and use it as I should,
Living an impossible dream to make music as long as I could,
Now as I see through the veil and channel as I do,
I know I'll be understood,
Understood even greater, when the music is brought to the public,
It may seem like a dream that showed up,
To others just a stroke of good luck.

The one in the vault of my soul is hidden up high; you need a ladder and tippy toes to find,
My Love helps me keep it there, she knows where my soul hides,
Traveling through time on a violet rainbow train, that violet flame,
Changing the world and ready to make music again,
You can help bring the song lyrics and the messages meant for the artists,
You can be on team Musique and be instrumental in getting it started,
A new way of making music.
I already learned I was guided, when I was alive,
In my past life as Musique, I was in the flow of the violet flame all the time,
I didn't mean to play so hard, musicians usually hit their mark,
If I could do it over I would move music-makers out of the dark,

Into the spotlights on stage,
Thank musicians more for all they gave,
They put their hearts and souls into their work,
If I ever pushed too hard or acted like a jerk,
I am sorry and I love them,
If I could do it over I would give each a hug,
A hug and look them in the eye and share all my love,
Because music opens the portal for you to feel the rising dove,
The Holy Spirit, the peace and the glory,
How everything fits into this story,
Soon to be part of a new edition,
To elevate people into heaven,
The heavenly vibe is the Love vibration,
Healers, warrior messengers, getting ready to go to battle of zapping out fear,
Show others trusting intuition and following your heart gets you here,
Into the higher frequency energy, where miracles show up on time,
The music, the messages to My Love, the lyrics and the rhymes,
Come from a much higher 5th Dimensional plane even 7D and higher sometimes,
For you - each of you - the answers you seek are always on divine time.

Letter to the Drum Master

I hear a funky tune,
Coming from inside of you.
Be an inspiration to others sharing visions from your soul and know,
Deep down inside there is rhythm in the earth,
The galaxies that surround have heavens still giving birth,
One cannot fathom a great expanse of love, like we see,
For on the other side we are as happy as can be,
Drumming to the energy.

I see a drummer writing down a beat,
There is a steel guitar in a case by this drum master's feet,
Doesn't use it often but knowing it's there draws me near,
In my drum master's heart I wish to always remain, my loveliest friend so dear.
I am so proud of this lovely soul, give this message through you from me.
It's Musique, drum master there's more for us in your destiny,
You can help us amplify the mission and shine a big spotlight,
For this plan comes from heaven from other lifetimes,
Past contracts that I have made, soul plans from the other side.
Oh, it's about as colorful as you can imagine, a violet flame all around,
With you and My Love and Katie channeling, we'll be knocking them down,
One by one every soul will be swept back up on their feet,
Out of the way you go if you aren't in line with Musique.
I am here to take a mic stand,
I feel imprisoned in the studio with others making plans,
The master of my domain I have always been,
What some are doing is full of sin.
Let the dreams of more money go,
Where we go the money always flows,
It comes from the way we elevate the world,

The truest intentions in our souls.
Don't be sad, drum master, know it's me, I am with you on radio shows,
You can talk about me with any name,
But really what My Love has learned and Katie, my channel, is I am really St. Germain,
The Ascended Master who came back on a mission with my twin flame,
My Love.

Now I see you looking in the mirror thinking what did he just say?
You'll find out soon enough why you are in the plan,
What God has in store for you and what to tell the band.
They can fill the sky with diamond light and wishes to play again.
I have a vision to teach others how the music never comes from your head,
The rhythms and the lyrics come from the soul, from angels and guides, so instead,
Thinking how much, how fast, how long....just groove,
Let it come through,
Never stop believing in you.
Be considerate of the music's need to come out when it's ready,
Ask your Spirit Guides for help and you will be rockin' steady.
Time escapes me on the other side; I could produce and jam all night.
Remember when your cymbal fell and rolled off out of sight?
Well, that kind of shit doesn't happen up in heaven. Ha! The music's perfectly alive.
Thank you for the times we sat on a log and helped each other cry,
You were finished playing and I had to dry my eyes,
I was so proud of you, you made it all happen, a dream come true.
Please know how much I care sweet friend, how much I love you.
Now go and tell the others I am reaching out to them soon.

The Song Is The Key

Experience is everything,
Know how to dream,
Be a delight, learn how to sing,
You need more pitch,
It goes a little something like this.
Ohhh it's gonna shake,
Your chords may feel like they may break,
Something inside of you knows how to elevate.

[Chorus]
The song is the key,
The music is the dream,
We've been here before,
Find the key and now the dream,
Find the key to your dream.

Songs that never leave your mind,
Ask for help and you will find,
Sitting at a piano, even if you're blind,
The key, the music, comes to you every time.

The song is the key,
The key is the dream,
Expand the rhythm and you will see,
The chords flowed through to me,
I always played with the possibility,
The song is the key,
The music is the dream,
Coming true for you, I'll show you how it's supposed to be.

The dream is the key,
Find the key and you'll see,
The music takes flight and unexpectedly,
You're in the flow, in the pocket and drums beat,
Now the guitar and strings feel the heat.

Music Therapy

Feeling inspired to lay down my magic guitar,
Sit at the bar for a while as the server counts tips from a jar,
To look around at other people without them noticing me,
Let me stir my drink in deep thought wondering how life would be.

[Chorus]
Live in the moment, let daydreams float away,
Live in the moment, be grateful for today,
Live in the moment, make your mark here right now,
Live in the moment, let the music show you how.

If I didn't have fortune and fame, what would I do next?
I think I'll try porn star, no, but something to do with sex,
Maybe I'll be a therapist making people's sex lives better,
When you both come home from work you can't wait to be together.

Yes, I'll give you all the passion back in your relationship,
You'll go down on each other like there is nothing to it,
I'll be in the business of making sure you all feel so good,
With each other and yourselves you will all be understood,
There will be more laughter and pleasure,
You'll be thanking me for changing your life,
You find the fun and joy that makes us feel so alive.

The bartender leans over the counter to me and says,
Hey you want another?
The bar door opens to the bright outside,
There is my chauffeur,
Says, it's time to go,
It's time for you to play another show.

As I walk out, I smile at a couple who is kissing,
They look up and say, "oh my God, it's you," and whisper, "we make love to your music."
As I swing the bar door closed letting in blinding light,
They yell out, "thank you, your music forever changed our lives!"

Our Life When I Needed the Road

It's a spiritual thing for you to see,
See your guides embracing you and for you to believe,
There's another vibration to be and other places to go,
Time to go on with the show,
Time to step up and be the one you want to be,
Without the hate and wondering if I am complete.
Know you have this and know you are alright,
Something you think about every night.
As you complete your goals and know you are there,
It won't come easier; you are already here.
Please share the following note,
It's one My Love knows I wrote.
Now is not the time to love me, it's not time to yet, don't,
Time to share my feelings, even if you won't,
Don't be that way, just say what you mean,
Tell me something spiteful like I messed up your dream,
In an instant you run, you climb to the door,
Scare off the pigeons on the roof floor,
Inside of me I wanted to say goodbye to you,
You came back in and brought our child with you,
Before hitting the road, I knew I had to say goodbye,
A nightmare we were living, both wanted to die.
I didn't feel the same after that, I had to move out and move on,
Nothing compares to your knowing and feeling like love is gone,

I didn't give up on you, you gave up on God's grace,
For a time until I saw you again and kissed your face,
As you stood by the door in a giant, tattooed place,
No denying I needed you more, I had no time to waste.
It wasn't an hour before you left and had a plan to go back home,
I went to your door and felt all alone,
It was in spite of the things we've done that I made a pact to let you go,
Be with the one I needed at the time who would let me know,
I was needed and wanted and could give and let go,
Give myself a break and slip back into the show.
I needed the road.

Road to Music

Oh, it didn't take long before I knew, you're the one that I'd do,
Shots with on the lonesome highway to the next town and show,
To music heaven on the road,
Where we play through the hours on the bus,
Work like dogs 'til someone makes a fuss,
Behind the stage we pull up and get down,
Down to the music, down to the love,
Down to the partying and sound above,
The stage, the mics, the seats and through my soul,
The crew unloads and dancers flow,
On to the stage for the show,
Where lights and pyrotechnics glow.

[Chorus]
The road to music, like a long embrace,
Road to music, a sweet escape,
The road to music, oh, oh I can't wait.

You feel the mood start to rise,
To a higher vibration in the sky,
Build your body's strength to carry on,
Deliver another epic performance,
For the fans, it's so important,
To impact their lives,
Like you've meant the songs for them all this time.

[Chorus]

You've paid your dues,
Now let the rhythm take you,
To the place where you and heaven shine through,
All the lyrics they all love,
Bring all you got and bare your soul,
Express your heart, make them feel all you know,
How to let it all go,
They need your songs,
They need your grace,
They need to feel you're with them through this escape.

[Chorus]

After the encores you'll always remember,
Like they will too, that you made a difference,
For one another during the concert,
As the music beats go on to the next city,
You spread the love that you're given,
As time passes your soul starts to feel complete.

Freedom Plays the Road

Disillusioned and alone in my world,
All I'm missing is my baby, my girl,
Tired of conforming,
Tired of keeping quiet,
When my views aren't accepted, get pushed back into hiding,
Brighter place to be is on the road with me,
Time to shake it down,
Filling music shows in town after town,
Jump on a bus, rush to the plane,
Sleep for a while, do it all over again,
Drink power drinks, jam with the band,
Get ready for a new set, been wanting to jam,
Just want to play free,
No time constraints, letting go to be me,
Escaping to the energy within the songs pocket,
Never thinking for a moment, only feelings I can rock it,
Different kind of love, levitating, feeling in your heart,
Losing yourself, bring it back and now you start,
The band going into what feels like a dream, floating, and flying on the music,
Through the air above, the fans never getting used to it,
Rocking the night away, funking it up,
Drum solos, guitar shredding, and keyboards fill my cup,
Not much more to be thankful for than all this God-given love.

Shine On (In the Music)

Shooop, Ahh, Oh, Shooop, Ahh,
Shooop, Ahh, Oh, Shoop, Ahh,
Steel guitars oh and drumming to the beat,
Triangles clanging and the music fills the street,
Beat box bumping, bumping hips and spinning feet,
Oooh, ahh, rise up, shine on, feel the heat.

[Chorus]
Shine on,
In the music,
Shine on,
In the rhythm that's fine,
Shine on,
In the music,
Shine on,
In the sound divine,
Shine on,
In the music,
Shine on in the cadence that's mine.

Sizzling like the snare catching tempo off the wood,
Thumping your fingers on your desk and on your hood,
Rockin' it, shaking it, making music last all night,
Using anything you got to let your rhythm take flight.

Jamming on buckets, on pans, and pencils on a book,
The bigger the book the better the jam, one note was all it took,
For my voice to find the pocket in a song the whole world shook,
Butterflies filled up stomachs and goosebumps filled every arm,
Everyone was jamming, then slid in my magic guitar.

[Bridge]
Shine on in the music,
Feel it in your soul,
Shine on in the music,
In music you're never alone,
Shine on in the music,
Between the notes,
Where I am, I'm in the music,
Dancing within the moment where you let go,
That's the pocket, the transport to the other side.

[Chorus]

Magic Power In Music

An approach to music from the other side,
Working through you on this miracle ride,
Where the spirit world brings good things we could never imagine,
Like sliding down rainbows that must be science fiction,
It's not on the other side, where heaven is for most,
It's like the beaches in Bermuda that sparkle and glow,
Grows peace for all ages, I want you to know.

[Chorus]

Magic power in music,
Meant for all to hear and see,
Magic power in music,
This song's meant for you and me,
Magic power in music,
Time to rise, time to sing,
Magic power in music,
Oh, Oh, my love is free.

You may share my world as it is now,
Where I see everything from behind the golden veil,
In a flash of a light we come to you—exhale,
Breathe in the love surrounding you now,
It's sparkling all around.

A brilliant light, love meant to grow through you and out,
To millions of people needing the message Spirit shouts,
Songs of connecting will erase the doubt,
A world beyond Earth exists with power,
Gives a perfect eternity that starts with you right now.

What a wonder I never noticed your magic before,
If I can feel it this much, I know you can feel it more,
Accept heaven's help and bring your heart to the battle,
We're going to war with judgment, unforgiveness,
Win over souls that are rattled,
We'll shake the true spirit of life back into them through magic lyrics,
One can wait for a sign, and this is it, this is your super spirit.

Write words from your soul in the flow.

Chapter 3

Trusting Spirit Guides Through Archangel Gabriel, The Divine, and Musique's Life

Whether you've been opening the book to jump around or reading straight through, Chapter 3 brings everyone deeper into the message of trust - trusting the flow, trusting yourself in the flow, and trusting Spirit Guides.

The energy vibration of Chapter 3 elevates to a higher frequency with Archangel Gabriel and The Divine coming through to channel insights on what's happening and words of encouragement for the writer and reader learning the process. Don't be surprised if you start to feel sleepy or a gentle calmness. Higher frequencies of energy can calm your nervous system down or ramp you up with excitement, if there's something specific connecting with your mind and soul. Pay attention to your senses and how you may feel.

Musique helps us feel into the flow through his channeling by portraying more stories about his music experiences, his Spirit Guide journey, and teaching us to trust the signs our guides provide.

The rhythm and guidance continues to build about us stepping into a new elevated energy. Throughout Chapter 1 to 3, the Spirit Guides began dropping lyrics about our personal expansion occurring. Your ascension and expansion is happening while you're reading the book and in your own life now, whether you feel it or not. Would you like to have an awareness of what's happening within you and around you, so you can navigate your life more effortlessly? That's where your Spirit Guides come in, to assist you in your expansion and leveling up.

Your new life of experiencing the frequency of heaven (the other side) on Earth is here, it's always been here, but now it is easier to achieve. With more light pouring into the earth than any other time in history which places us in a higher vibration, it will be easier than ever before to connect with your Spirit Guides in the higher frequencies. When there is more light present than darkness, as is the case now, darkness gets pushed out and into the light for it to be seen and removed. Where we are headed, especially for the younger generations, working with Spirit Guides will one day be understood and accepted as essential to our purpose.

Archangel Gabriel's Vision: Believe You Matter

You can do anything. It is up to you to trust and believe in yourself,
We do and we will help you. Spirit is with you now and always.
It's inspiring to see you work on yourselves,
We see you; we hear you; we are with you.
Now Archangel Gabriel will take over, as you find your rhythm in your creativity,
Inspiring the world and others that life is meant to be,
Fun-filled with miracles, go on and trust,
Archangel Gabriel has fear-slashing faith to expand your heart,
Do what you do best,
Share your vision, eternity of life is available, you are safe,
Your anxiety wants to control,
You don't need it anymore,
It's gone forever, step into your power,
We are with you now and forever,
You cannot do anything wrong,
Nothing bad will happen to you, that's all behind us now.
Now breathe and be patient as the storm within
is all daisies and butterflies ready to come flowing,
Into the people you least expect,
You speak to them, to the power of music,
The book is a passage to the other side,
Believe you matter and learn to see heaven anytime,
You have the passage within the pages,
Inspires and aspires and celebrates the ages,
For in heaven, there is so much more to see,
As Spirit grows stronger around you and me,
Mystical wonder appears before your eyes,

We will come to you in the dark, you will see us there with light,
As a feeling of wind whispers lovely, sweet things only your guides would know,
Be you and begin again by working easily and grow,
Expand. Don't be afraid. Fear is fake and trickery. It is a trick,
Be careful of your thoughts. Thoughts fuel the fire of what is,
Think of what you want, need, shall have forever more,
This is how it works and always works,
Those that think the good thoughts have powerful good and expanse,
You are part of the power of the universe,
Meant for you without struggle, no more struggles, no more feeling worse,
Like you did in the lives gone by, believe and always believe,
The power of the universe shines and releases all you do not need.
In you, through you, like going to church but church is always with you.
Those tears are meant to cleanse your souls,
Start anew and be the change as Spirit calls,
On a new train ride to the other side; it's how we roll.
I can see you in the meditation meadow as the trees sway,
Welcome Musique to you again.

How Musique Met His Maker Before Guiding The Lyric Creator

Wishing there was a time when I could sit by the fire,
Remember the days of patience, pain, and desire,
Deep in the heart I knew it wasn't right,
I stepped away to face another day,
The twinkling in her eye made my heart skip a beat,
I fell to my knees and ran to the street,
It didn't matter anymore I had inspired her to go,
I threw on my robe and I headed out the door,
To the one place I knew she'd be—in the garden on her hands,
Waiting for her joy to return, like the eyes of a desperate fan.
I couldn't leave her alone, there wasn't anything I could do,
I'd see her in the morning and try to wipe away her blues,
With my songs of love and rhythm and grace,
For in the night hours those are haunting, but in the day you feel the grace.

When I crashed down to the floor,
It was not what I had in store,
As I experienced the light of heaven engulf my spirit,
Soaring to God's feet, I was brought with a boom,
His bright light around me and not happy about what I'd consumed.
Into the fog I drifted, and I looked back for my life ending too fast,
The plan was God's now, so I knew I wasn't bad,
I was forgiven for my choices in that life and my change of fate,
It was sealed by my soul contract, and I walked through heaven's gate.

What a miracle! A majestic wonder!
My eyes looked up and gazed out far and wide,
In the distance there are angels and light beings flying by,
They take you into the mystic where all the legends are, you know where they go,
See them one by one saying hello.

I loved my life down on the earth plane but my rhythm I lost it, so you see,
That is where you come in for me,
To work my rhythm through you to see,
As you bring it to life you will share with the world how life can be,
When you know there is a heaven and we
communicate from the other side giving you signs,
Love and hope for miracles by your side.

An experience I hope for you and everyone who loves to write songs and beats,
If you can experience light in your purpose, no one can compete,
With your energy and your soul and the rhythm that you seek,
In life and in your songs, and in your beauty, believe,
It's me. It's Musique, tell them and they'll believe.
Don't be afraid,
I'll explain through your writing, they feel my spirit without a mistake,
Can't get over the magnificence on the other side for you to share,
Meant for the spirits of all the world,
Elevating our streets, churches, alley ways, dives and corner stores,
Bring the message to everybody; know the message is yours,
We'll help you birth it and give all it needs to grow,
Now believe in yourself, you've got it, let the rhythm flow and flow.
I see you in the rhythm; it's not complicated, this is who you are,
Share your body and soul with the world, the artists will know which guitar,
To play with your music, they'll know the rhythm and key you mean,
Find your power in the words only—that's all you have to do and believe,
Musicians know the sound,

Time to do it, the time is now,
We'll help you; you'll see, we swear on heaven's grave if there was one
but there's not, so we will swear on love, because in the end,
We grow more love and expand,
Into the depths of the light there is no end,
Power that grows and goes on forever gets more miraculous the more you rise,
Into the feeling that is pure light.

Pure splendor. Wonder why we don't know this before we get here to the other side?
Here is where you come in, to help others experience the ride,
Now into the mystic you should fly,
Tell My Love I love her and I'm with her all the time,
Show her the song about the garden and the statue that was mine,
You will meet her some time, everything will be alright,
Don't be embarrassed,
My Love will find your music,
It will be like you were long, lost cousins, when you two finally meet.
Don't give up before the miracles happen, magic's right over here,
I know you feel me, a tingly touch upon your hair,
The feel of your energy reaching upwards, touching 5D light from there,
Your light is tall and bright and expansive,
Down into your deepest soul power, through your heart is where it goes.
Allow conviction of your heart's desire to lead the way,
The stars are never out of reach, they are constellations in your DNA,
The same matter that makes up your brain, your neurons and your pain,
How you use it all and let it go makes each of us unique,
Now spill it over, let the words run off into their own beat,
Let the flow take you over and enjoy the experience and mystery,
Share your love with others. It will be easy as pie, you shall see,
We are helping you from heaven. You have a spiritual posse so don't freak,
Nothing to worry about, you feel the power, we take care of the rest,
You have more power in your words to change the world for the better,

Impacting many souls who need to cry out to feel discovered,
With you they will finally see,
Life is not about the controlling authority,
Fake celebrity figures in the world who made you think they are all great,
Life is about living your dream,
Believing in yourself and knowing you are 100% complete,
As you are, as a human, without the fancy stuff and boats and cars,
God wants you to have all that, if it's your desire and spreads love like fire,
Let it all go in your heart at least,
It will show up when it's meant to be,
Feel the feelings you want to feel, when you know you've done the right thing,
I think you've got it now. I'll leave you to it. I love you, my sister. I love you, my sweet.
See you in the morning after you've had some sleep,
I'll share your good news with your Grandpa Charlie,
He is here waiting for you to succeed,
He needs you to finish the songs so he can get his time to teach,
How to write the book of your dreams.
Ha! Like Musique's isn't the one, these lyrical rhymes of mine,
To make millions experience expansion in their lives,
Live it up large, give to others before your time,
Before your time is up, to come with us into the stars and light,
We love you, now goodnight.

For Musique's Revolution

The vault is the solution,
Where you got soul, you have grace,
You got rhythm,
A warm embrace,
Into the darkness we must shine,
Believe it is our time,
To be the one that knows how the story goes,
This is Musique. Feel the rhythm take control.

I didn't want this to happen, it's a course from Spirit,
I thought I'd be in heaven having fun and that's it.
Great Spirit came to me and said, *it is not over,*
I need you to write more songs, believe,
You can do this from the other side with me,
We'll find Katie to shed light and pick up your energy
vibe in the song that is meant for all,
Time to surprise the world and let it take off.
I didn't expect it either. I knew I'd find you and strength to bring it through,
No denying you have class to shake to,
I go on believing in what I can't ignore,
Life is meant to feel good, those feelings don't ignore,
The more fun it is, the more it is meant to be,
Feel the fun come through and trust that it is me, I am Musique.

I feel the spiritual revolution and it exudes,
Oh, uh-oh, hold on to one another, it is about to get crude,
Nothing like that here, all sexual love is beautiful in heaven,
A connection to the Divine Masculine and Feminine,
A vibe from everlasting life, from Jesus and Mary Magdalene,

They taught the power of love on the planet,
A reason why fear-rulers wanted Jesus dead,
Jesus's soul partner was as powerful as He,
Rulers of fear didn't like it, you see,
Because by giving birth to more love like them,
Mary M. was more powerful than those fear-spreading men.
Bringing life into the world through child and grace,
It's all a miracle when you know She, the Divine Feminine, saves the human race.

Don't give up on the desire to make others feel alive,
They know me and feel the truth that inspired,
You coming all this way with a purpose to give to them,
It's all for them, for the world, now let's see who all comes,
Doesn't second guess what their soul is telling them,
Love is not meant to be easy when your fear is controlling fun.

Back to my band, I used to say that I have you in me, here in my heart and my guitar,
As I danced to drum masters, there is no mistaking their beauty I'd say, their beauty shakes our core,
I'll never forget band members laughing on the floor,
As I tuned my guitar in my undies like, hey, I'm a star,
We laughed until it was time to play,
It was an act we put on but knew,
It was coming from someplace else, like the angels approved,
Our songs the wilder they got as we flowed through,
Every town, shaking it down, and raising vibes,
I always looked out at the audience with a shyness in my eye.

Then it was My Love who said to me, you are like a smoking gun,
Guards packing heat took care of you and on to the next town,
I would talk to her, discuss taking our child on tour and play as we knew,
It felt like magic coming through,
I didn't know how much she hurt. I figured she did,
I was the one trapped in the hell the sorrow made,
It was the music that brought me back to where I always needed to be,
With her in my heart I always feel complete,
I do want her to know I see her in that robe,
By the pool or doing laundry or getting ready for a show,
Sitting outside in silence and wishing I would know,
I did love her more than life, more than my own,
I felt her near me even after we said goodbye,
We were meant for each other, we've come from the other side,
Together, many times, one was with so many kids,
I thought we'd have in this past lifetime, but most of my children are lyrical music.

My songs were my children, I birthed them through every verse,
Loved giving them life through others, it was a blessing and a curse,
I couldn't stop writing, I made them love me, all my children, they are my songs,
I knew you longed for that and that's when you came along.
I feel the power of the world starting to make a shift,
It's people like you that trust the crazy vibe and make this gift,
A gift for the world to share, now you are birthing and planting seeds just like me,
Give this to the world and let us see what they believe,
Where Spirit shines the light, all planned miracles make an entrance,
It's coming, it is time, oh yes, this is Musique.

A Message from The Divine About Our Light

The spirit within us is a natural being of light,
Surrounding us in everything we do and all we transform,
There is magnificent force between you and the light,
A force unknown to man, a light like no other,
The light sees through you to the Divine Father and Mother,
Brings salvation on all the land,
For in eternal darkness there is nothing,
In eternal light there is awe and grandeur of the highest magnitude for all.
Return to the light over and over and it gets stronger,
As I am in you and you are in me, for all to see, hear, be, and believe,
It is transparent to me, how you believe and what you do and say,
Being all you can be, you break down energy barriers for all who come before you and who pass your light.
The light is stronger than any one human or thing that is elevated higher than you,
There is a higher level for everyone to reach,
It escapes your mind, I know,
You were there many times before,
We remember those things in our dreams,
Believe in those things of unconditional love behind the veil,
A gracious feeling is knowing you are here now,
The feeling brings peace to the whole realm and the stars,
By being the loving person you truly are,
You each bring light and everlasting love to the world,
As the Divine, and being what is necessary for all to live through you,
Be you and experience everything you see, need, and understand,
Everything's meant to be the most miraculous it could be in this lifetime,
Quite a peaceful experience to have and to hold and love,
Know you are at peace, as you are with Musique.
He is for you and with you, and I brought you together,

To be each other's womb, create, to feel each other's heart,
To bring the world a new passageway to the other side,
Together, we will change the world vibration,
In that moment, I will be there guiding you through writing.

In the experience you bring, you shall elevate souls to their highest dream,
They will know it as soon as they see and feel our work.
Each one of you are light—that bright light, always and forever, I am your God, your love,
Your peace and passion and everything you dream of,
You and me and everyone together, we are all one,
I believe in you and everything you do,
We expand as we are supposed to,
Let's expand this energy and bring in more light, watch how it rises to the next frequency and realm,
Bring people to the next level and dimension,
Even more than they have ever been,
Coming soon, so soon you will see and receive, you shall receive. It's all about receiving.
For you just receive and receive, receive and receive.
Believe and believe, believe and believe,
Faith is the cornerstone of everything, my dear. Just breathe.
Believe. Expect miracles to happen as they do. Oh, those miracles.

The Divine's Time
To Share Encouraging Words Of Why

You can't stop the automatic flow when Spirit enters the room,
Precisely on-time perfection is what God has in store,
Nothing stops us from sharing God's grace,
The Divine puts our spin on it to heal our race,
Our human race of love, we are all love,
No darkness starts us out,
Bring love to the next level,
Think about the times you didn't know what to do,
All the sudden there was the answer right in front of you,
Magic is too short a word for the experience it grows within,
It plants a seed into the evolution,
Growth of the universe, and no one can sow the seed
like you and like me, because together our cosmic energy,
Fills a gap in space and time and grows the universe,
The way God needs and wants.
Expand into the light beyond the light, the infinity for each of you to share,
A meditation will get you there,
Mystic moments with Spirit launch you farther beyond the sphere,
Divine light of love glows like a search light into the sky,
Below your feet and out of your heart aligned,
With what is meant for your soul before your body dies,
Think of it as a lost expression, a song sung within a different key,
Grasp that this is all for your survival through eternity,
Not everyone gets to the other side so easily,
People like you are rare, you see,
I sent you channels, a shaman and priestess to discover your healing face,
It is serious when you can write this way,

As my love guides you over the page,
Down and down like a book of songs creating with Musique that way,
I never before did this this way. I do it differently with all you see,
If Spirit can choose what you are meant to do,
Don't you think I can get you awards and money, too?

When your efforts are effortless, flow takes over your Divine power,
Sheer energy to finally grab your desire,
I think of rhythms of the finest hour.
You know the best and wondrous lyrics the world remembers for all the years is their simple way,
They tell a story and brighten up a day,
A miracle of inspiration, a toe tap of joy so profound,
You are all uniquely you, that means everyone who is built for sound,
The words that rhyme,
Coming to your mind,
That is me, Spirit, through your Spirit Guides,
Filling your head and heart with the beats of rhymes,
Rhythms from angels passing by,
I still have my story to tell and with you we shall bring it to the world stage,
Go and express the lyrics you made,
You can tell the story of Musique or keep it to yourself, but you'd be doing a disservice not to explain,
How the channeling filled your brain,
Their hearts and spirits will want more of Musique and your light-filled words,
I think you will shine on through and through,
A box of rain with light was sent to you from here,
On the other side, and for you we cheer,
Because I feel your body wanting to heal,
I give you a miracle of love. Believe and feel,
I am with you now and give you the miracles you seek,
Stronger than you have felt before, I am always here.
Be ready, don't be scared of all that comes your way,

No rushing, feel your way with ease.

Star beings share a wave as they pass by above me,
They are not bad, they are good and strong,
Have a familiar passion for what you do and love,
Be patient as Spirit gives you what you want and need,
I am here for you now and it is free.
Amen. Love conquers the seven seas,
Begin again as you need,
Learn to go to the next level of love,
I could go on and on for I am God, as I feel you know,
Time to fly to share the good news,
You will be making it back here as a writer of books and songs,
I feel a loneliness call,
So I must go to take off,
I've done a million things while we've talked,
Now on to the moon and the sun,
More work to be done.
Imagine how you want to be, and the rest will follow, follow me.
I love you, Katie,
Be good to yourself. It's me in that heart with you; you've got this, my sweet.

Creators Create With Light
According to The Artist and The Divine

Into the dawn we must go,
Without a thought of what we know,
Trying to collaborate to share the magic words,
A new dawn, a new age literally changing where your spirit flows,
Bring your essence of what Spirit gave you, it is time to show,
The world wouldn't be the same without any of you,
Experience the end of darkness, while the light carries you through,
I feel a kiss, the doves, and the violet flame as we share
my story from the other side, your light shows you care,
It couldn't have been without the death of my loved one,
Why I am here so soon, before I was meant to come.
Feels a little bit like swimming through waves of energy,
At a blink of an eye I see you, try harder and you will see me.
Feels a little bit like making the colors in rainbows,
Harnessing light for it to grow,
When you see sparkles that is us within our energy shield,
Grows bigger as we expand our spirits to the next level, on and on we feel,
Time to get up off your feet,
Listen to the music steal the beat
of your heart and grab those thoughts,
A new day makes it right all along,
I will follow you everywhere your heart goes,
Follow you until you finish and go on the road,
Get what belongs to you, the love on stage, glory in the studio,
Deliver miracles and madness of lyrical love,
Process and experience the flow,
Writers write, artists paint,
In their minds and with palette, pen, piano, and pain.

Spirit Guide Signs To Get Back in the Flow
Author's Note on the Channeling Session:

Before going for a walk on the beach I heard, "take a notebook and pen with you," so I grabbed them, as I headed out the door. I was walking on the West Beach of Kiawah Island, South Carolina, when many signs and messages appeared from my Spirit Guides. First, an osprey flew overhead. Next, I saved a live starfish that was beached on the sand and placed it back in the ocean. After the starfish, I found a white feather that appeared right in front of me on the sand. White feathers began appearing everywhere in my life, when I began channeling. The final sign or message on the beach from my Spirit Guides was one of Musique's songs started playing on my phone by itself. I hadn't been listening to music. A message update appeared on my phone screen that read, "you are offline." When the song started playing, it stopped me in my tracks, as I was about to leave the beach. I turned around, sat down on the sand, and as soon as I put pen to paper this is what came through:

You can escape yourself with me,
You can deliver your miracles amidst a shining sea,
You can experience bliss,
You can create another kiss,
You can express yourself and needs,
Relax, think happy thoughts and breathe,
Don't be surprised of a magic flight taking place,
You are in heaven now surrounded by grace,
Such a beautiful feeling to know we exist,
I created this one you can't resist.

Dive deep into heaven,
Surrounded by seven,
Shall a majestic bird fly over, that's our sign to you,
You are guided, watched over by more than a few.
Interesting isn't it? Life is easy,
When you ignore the media and the crazies,
I inspired a writer,
I found you again to take us higher,
Don't be embarrassed by your gift,
Cherish how many people this will lift,
Again with those eyes of the soul,
Your life purpose is full of gold,
It awaits you now that you finally let go,
What took you so long?

We had to make it come through your husband, Lee,
That was us talking through Lee, so your mind and heart would see,
We have been waiting for you a long time,
Ready? It's time to shine.
Let it all go. Money will come,
Follow the excitement. Have and create fun,
Together we will make a fresh start,
Discover more life in lyrics together, not apart,
Life expands and the world grows with peace,
Nothing can stop what is coming, no more fear, no more disease,
A challenge for you is to forget the past,
Remember you are in this lifetime to create something that lasts.
Send a bright star, a gift of unconditional love,
Like I said, I am human, and I am a peace dove,
I drop down on my knees to honor, anchor into the earth,
A new golden age upon us, much more to birth
in you and for all who came here, we have said it before many times,

You all chose to do this together, remember who you are in this rhyme.
Into the light I expand, as the tide fills you up.
Any moment now a ring on the phone fills your cup,
A cup of blessings and the plan shifting fast,
A new day to do this collaboration that lasts,
Anxious no more, a new life finally appears,
Rediscover who you are – each of you – without fear.
A light in the studio flickers at night,
Me getting under their skin to do what is right,
Lasting not that much longer, a few of them will turn out their light,
When you are building from your past life,
Make an entrance to save the day,
No less with My Love,
The grace of God is on display,
A heavenly wish from me is for you to simply be,
The love you are and have always been,
In our past lives in galaxies far and near,
A brief moment in time, a blip,
Sit back and take a sip,
Drink of the energy the life force gives to everyone,
Some can guide and harness it like the light of the sun,
A shift is happening now,
Look at the clouds,
The queasy feeling is us bringing you back down,
As you get planted back on the ground,
Look inside your heart,
Celebrate this beautiful start,
Share this with the world. This is your art.
Dig it? Believe it.

How to Connect with the Other Side

In the distance you will see us, as we gaze through the veil of light,
A flash of light and colors so bright,
We will watch you and don't freak out; it will happen.
Expand your light to connect with your guides,
Available to you now, and for us it is time,
Open your eyes with your third eye wide,
Relax into it and be still, nothing to think anymore,
Let go of preconceived notions that you know what to look for,
We are not the form that you think,
We are light and love and bright and tall with colors,
We are beauty in all forms,
An expression from God, the Universe we all honor,
Be open to the light. Yours is strong and brave,
We have been waiting for this time on your journey,
We will hear your calling.
Life had gone on for some time into the darkness,
Your path longed for us,
Now in the light you all are, a true miracle to watch,
Believe in you. We believe in you all the time,
Our destiny is to be with you always on both sides,
With the realms of the ages too soon to know what lies ahead,
Spirit has miracles for us to expand,

For you to dwell and be free,
A new life is here and awake you shall be,
Remember our love-light is bright and tall and sparkly,
With colors, with light, you may see,
Blue light coming down and that is safe, blue light is your friend,
With you to guide you to the end,
Softly it will get bright in your right vision now,
We are up above but not far, always up, never down,
Uncertainty isn't necessary, that is something to let go of,
Believe, have faith, and connect to our love.

Rock Your Soul

I didn't break my bones, but it felt like I broke my heart,
Out of nowhere the universe gives you a fresh start,
What you do with it sets you apart,
Into the cocoon your body goes to heal,
Out you'll come again with new wings to feel.

[Chorus]
Don't give up, it's time to believe,
Don't give up, choose happy, choose to heal,
Rock your soul and be free,
Rock your soul, let it free,
Rock your soul, let it believe.

I believed I was saved,
I carried on and felt brave,
I knew I could have it worse, but no more,
It's the last time my body was this sore,
Count your blessings, what you're grateful for.

[Chorus]
[Bridge]
Flat on my back—don't give up,
My heads down in my lap—don't give up,
My body hurts to carry on—don't give up,
But my soul's automatically writing this song.

[Chorus]
Rock your soul, let it free,
Rock your soul, let it believe,
Rock your soul and be free.

Level Up

Rhythm sounds like:
Boom chee boom, ba chu ba chu ba, boom chee boom, ba chu ba chu boom chee boom

As the darkness turns to light,
Experiences pass us by,
I dream of a day when I can feel alive,
To be who I want to be and celebrate love,
Remember the songs, hear the woo of the dove,
An excellent choice to make is one when I see,
You choosing to be the one to set my spirit free.

[Chorus]
Level up, break through fear,
Level up, embrace, cut fear,
Level up, enter the race,
Level up, do what you were meant to be,
Level up, leave the past behind,
Level up, don't dwell, spread the kind of love you need,
Level up, and believe it's all your spirit needs.

In the light of day, I receive your grace,
On a mountain top, a closer sun on my face,
Burns through to my heart and I climb to escape,
Don't give up on me, ain't no time to waste,
Into the dawn I feel the sun on my face,
Into the dawn I feel amazing grace.

[Chorus]

[Bridge]

Level up
Be the one
Level up
Here we come
Level up
You're the one
Level up
Have some fun
Level up
Don't engage
Level up
Feel good, no rage
Level up
Be full of life
Level up
Enjoy your life

I find a shelter to share my love,
I find a zillion times I felt you give it back to me,
I didn't know what to do first and I fell on my knees,
To give praise to Jesus that I had lasted this long,
It wasn't until I saw you there that I knew it all along,
I had this music in me, and I need to see your face,
I needed you to believe me and know this was the way,
The way of showing others they will have what it takes,
To jump up a level, level up and make miracles happen again.

[Chorus]

SET TWO

Divine Feminine Time

Chapter 4
Lyrics for My Love

Chapter 5
Sexy Songs and Lyrics About Ladies

Chapter 4

Lyrics for My Love

The day I began compiling the Channeled Writing for Chapter 4 about Musique wanting to reach his loved one, there was a dove that kept wooing in the tree outside my office window the entire morning. It was like listening to dove lyrics and noticing the rhythmic pattern in the notes. Then it dawned on me. I finally understood that like my Spirit Guides giving me a sign from the dove outside my window, Spirit Guides like Musique also try to reach loved ones and provide signs to people they co-create with. They have healing to give, messages to share, and wish to work with you for your personal expansion.

In the channeling with Musique in Chapter 4, the lyrics reveal that in a past life, Musique told his lover he would contact her in a very specific way from the other side. Chapter 4 shares Musique's mission. During the Channeled Writing process, lyrics came through about my past life connections to Musique with one of the missions within my soul contract being to come back as a writer, a cosmic scribe, to channel these lyrics and help him connect with you. If I've learned anything in this channeling process with Musique it's to follow his divine plan, or shit starts to go wonky real fast and obstacles begin showing up until I follow the guidance again. Letting Musique complete his mission of coming back as a Spirit Guide through lyrics is part of our divine plan together. As Musique and I expand by achieving this mission, the readers expand. We are all connected.

In respect for the laws, the original Channeled Writings have been edited to remove names, places, and words that may appear to be in reference to personal identity.

As you know through the love songs and lyrics you listen to, many of us have similar stories and experiences in our lives – the pain, the sorrow, the joy. I kept being pushed forward and guided by my Spirit Guides to not be afraid to share the Channeled Writing about Musique's love stories, because many people would relate to the lyrics as their own stories, and that there is a greater purpose meant to help heal others and elevate their personal connections.

Reaching My Love With Songs

You call on me and that's when I help,
I help you see that I've been here all this time,
You finally believe and listen to the rhymes,
The life in lyrics, the passion, the artistic rhythm and guitar,
Nothing can stop what is coming, you'll be awakened by the solar flare.
I want to whisper in your soul,
Trust the lyrics, trust the process, and go with the flow,
Sometimes we make you laugh, to release your mind's control.
I want you to get up and dance,
Express yourself, give it a chance.

Bring the expansion to me and my God-given soul,
Don't ask me anymore, I'm giving up control,
I'm taking the key and hiding it from all,
I'll leave it in the studio and scrap the code off the wall,
Think about the time I knew you would answer the call,
It was me and I was sending you codes,
With it came a book of notes,
You were to wait until I contacted you from heaven,
I would send a messenger, a way to connect us again,
You would compare what the messenger sent with what we had agreed upon,
You'll remember the time I said wear that pink robe outside by the hedge so long,
The song will come rushing back into you, the many songs,
We filled the vault together,
You will see the way through all of this, the story of one another,
Through the messenger that I send, we are in this together,
The pact we made in our lifetime is a divine plan to elevate the world,
Nothing can stop the divine plan, not for you, for me, or that baby boy or girl.
Dreams are envisioned upon a night star circling your bed,

A star that watches over you and lays upon your head,
A loving touch and graceful blessing to help the other ones around you see,
This isn't about what you think, it is about what your heart and soul feel,
Your heart knows if it is me,
Your soul knows the mission has only just begun,
Damn wait until you put moves to this feeling, that's when it gets fun,
Sugar Pop, that's what I would say,
Drinking from a glass of champagne or rosé,
Up on the top shelf to the left of the door and down a few rows,
There is a box and binder that has songs in there for you,
They are songs we channeled together and My Love will know what to do.
She has seen them before. She knows which ones I am talking about,
Sometimes she and I wrote at night and we had figured out,
How to channel like this automatic gift that you have,
We did it together and she'd see me doing it too. It was rad,
She could channel through moving,
I would channel through my music and producing,
Many songs in the vault of my soul, I know where they go,
I know who they are for,
I have said this a time before.

My Love has a grand piano, sometimes hears a key played or two,
She knows it's me but wonders why can't I just talk to her, but I do,
The more time for silence in your head,
The more time to listen and hear instead.

When the whole world wakes up and that will be soon,
After the real history is learned about everything like the moon,
You will be ready to help people with believing and receiving, both kids and adults,
None of this will be without results,
For anyone that has been guided to read this and align,
This guidance is coming to the world in the essence of time,

It is right on time for you from the Divine.
A collaboration with Spirit Guides for the new Golden Age to see,
Working together, collaborating is how you achieve,
The life and work of your dreams,
Follow the guidance, we will lead the way,
Listen to your heart not what others say,
Pay attention to how it feels. Does it feel good?
Oh, when it feels good is when your purpose is understood,
You can dance, you can write, play music, bring the messages to all,
You are together and that means you have answered our call.
Spirit soars, the galaxies expand their knowledge from us to you,
You are the vessels, the messengers, meant to share and bring energy through.

So in the end, we come through again and again,
No one worries of your intentions,
It is quite thoughtful and conscientious,
You are an automatic writer and channeler with special gifts,
To share, teach, inspire others, the world needs more of this.
You are teaching in your book, right now, right here,
See how we do things, my dear?
For thousands of years we have been on both sides,
My old friend from Ayers Rock, one of our past lives,
We stood on the mount together and helped each other out,
You were a brave chief, loud and powerful and your people, your tribe,
Honored and respected your every word, your high energy vibes.
We helped you with planting, irrigation, sewing, and technology,
To share with others you would lead and meet,
My galactic friends and me,
Took you to the heavens in our spaceships with us,
You saw how it all works,
It was before the time of Christ, the beloved Jesus.
How many lifetimes have we been together?

Five lifetimes with a mission every time to help one another,
Always some wild mission,
Out of the norm of how people did things,
Always required by God to push the envelope,
Out of the box, raise love higher, always a lofty goal,
For us the goals are always to help elevate the world to higher vibes,
Our pact remains to help each other from both sides.
One on Gaia or in the galaxies,
One from the other side, like me,
Behind the veil in the angelic realm,
With my Spirit Guide, Archangel Raziel.
Oooh, oooh, it's just getting good,
We still have so much more to give and receive,
To write. To dream. To be.
To share. To elevate. To sing.
To dance. Oh, to dance. Just wait and see.

More Than Words for My Love to Feel

Bring your beauty back to me,
Feel me in your arms, think about what you want to be,
Think about your time away,
Let me come in, let me make you see,
I am the one for you, you know you need me,
I need you to need me, to make a passion child, a love gift,
Aspire to give, to make an energy shift.
Expect miracles to happen, it's as if they are in front of you,
Align your spirit with mine and create and bring it through,
Right there within your reach, an absent thought brings me back to a place,
I knew before grace, a place with My Love at the ocean listening to Mace,
Maceo Ocean would have been the name, if I had won the name game.

An instinct in me knew something wasn't right,
You know that gut feeling, when your heart can fill instantly with fright?
You shake it off and smile and say,
Babe, it's gonna be okay,
For sure a feeling I'll never have again,
Saying goodbye to your loved ones, you knew,
This world wasn't meant for me and you,
Not walking on Gaia but on this magic side we will be,
For now let's help guide her to her destiny.

I fill a mountain of doves over you and release them in the air,
Here they come from me to you, and I believe, I know you care,
Grab these doves and give them a home—homes of the highest place,
Wait for the next one, it's a passion one, it will fly upon the charts and race,
To the top, the top of this place. That's magic, that is grace,
Bestowed upon all who hear, who listen and embrace,
A new way of thinking and believing; there is more to all of us, to Musique,
Musique is here; now be the one who accepts and celebrates,
Nothing for you to do but love my songs as my children,
Because in the end, there is no end,
I'm here with you and in heaven.
Believe. You will see.
A sparkle by the water bird feeder—that's me.

The Vault of My Soul

Violet passion came out of the room,
Someone else delivered the sonic boom,
Don't get all clever thinking you know me,
Passion fills fires of desires, lay next to me and you'll see.

Baby, remember when we were together, a storm took us into the ocean,
When I discovered your love potion,
It was like a supersonic truck hit me, when I discovered your love,
I didn't have enough time to rise above,
The chaos that was around me, sucking my life out, felt like a caged dove.

Now back to the vault of my soul,
A nice girl only comes around maybe once or twice, the true one does,
The one that finishes your thoughts,
At the same time says, you reading my mind?
A connection that not many find,
Oh baby, you inspired me to make life better,
For when the time came I wanted it to be forever.
It still is now, forever that is,
We can pick up where we left off in our great love moment,
Remember baby, you and me, we are heaven sent,
Now go inspire yourself to allow true love back into your heart,
I'm coming back, I have a light body, this is just the start,
A new day is coming for you, for me, for all the children saved in the world,
So many children have been saved,
Tens of thousands, millions maybe, of boy and girls.
Now back to you and me sweet thing,
Where did we leave off that last wonderful moment we had?
Oh yes, that's when I was going to be a Dad.

I'll always remember you sitting there with your legs up,
Wondering should I have more ice cream, just a little bit,
You moved through the room on your toes in that dynamite outfit,
Wishing you had a belly no more and a baby in your arms,
When I got up after watching you, to come over and keep you warm.

A warm embrace, a lover's face,
Let's get out of this place,
Just for a while,
Go somewhere in style,
To the beach or to the city,
Some place you love, always pretty,
I'm feeling dizzy,
That's what you said, and we sat on the couch,
I got worried and started to pout,
Didn't bite my nails but if I did this would be the time,
God guided us on, two souls carried by the Divine,
I didn't know how we put two feet in front of the other,
We did and we tried, we wanted to be together.
I love her more than anything, she is a spicy tamale,
Our angel is by your side, as you can see,
I know you see him with you, he's with you and me.

Now baby just listen to me, I know your powers better than most,
I am the light, the light being, a light body traveling from coast to coast,
I channel here and channel there, I work in the studio still and watch the plan,
Do things with my music, sometimes knock over a mic stand.
Oh my, where does the time go,
Is what I think when I look at all my music in my soul, like a vault,
Good Lord, I was working hard and in the flow, too dedicated to a fault.
To the illusion of the legacy, I am in control and protect my children, they are my songs,
As you know, that's why you came along,

The vessel, the channeler, the guide from the other side,
We'll share our past life stories, there is nothing to hide.
You keep going with the flow, that's what I did and you're learning from me,
You don't think. You simply receive.
I was great at receiving, stayed up all night receiving divine music to rock my soul,
Hopefully make the world a better place, that was my goal,
It still remains, as you know,
It's your mission too, to elevate as many people as we can,
Now go believe in yourself and don't give a damn,
What anyone thinks of your gift to connect on the other side,
Believe in your power, all of you, it's the best time to be alive.
You chose to be here at this time.

A time never experienced before,
Christ is coming back, I am too, wait until you see what's in store.

Be the vision we all seek,
Turn off the TV, go out in the street,
Step away from the brainwashing electronics and feel your heartbeat,
Your heart connects to us and that is when we meet,
I'll meet you by the hedge so long,
You will discover this love song,
It's about not giving up on love to focus on wrongs.

A spider came to me sad, because he lost his wife,
She was his queen, the master of his life,
As far as love goes she treated him with glowing praise,
As far as I can see a knight in shining armor was he in those days,
The pain kept them apart,
That's the message here, always follow your heart,
Don't give up on love, when it's too hard,
Turn your brain off, make a fresh start,
Forgive and release all that does not serve you,

Remember who you are in those best loving moments, that's your true blue,
The real essence of one another is when you are creating love,
Hearts filled with peace of the dove,
Don't get stuck in shame, guilt, or illusions of fear,
Fear is not real. Spread the word to those you love dear.

Now sweetie back to you, my everlasting twin flame divine,
Are you ready to say again you are going to be mine?
Well, I'll let you think about it, but no playing hard to get please,
There is a big mission to complete,
Need you on board with us, I love you, my sweet, Sugar Pop baby.

Open The Vault Without A Key

I see it in the vault up above the highest shelf in my heart,
A few secret songs no one knew but me from the start,
Now I am automatic writing my soul songs with you.
My Love will be flabbergasted, might hold her heart and mouth will gasp,
I always said I am coming back with class.
Who would have seen that it would happen this way,
No ghostly encounters, something that blows her spirit away,
Discovering how we work together now will eventually brighten her day,
No more sorrowful days for her, she'll learn more how to connect,
She is a sorceress of great power, an elevating spirit, her light direct,
She is on a new course,
One that may knock her off her horse,
Put her back on the path to her soul contract and divine plan,
One that involves working with light beings and this celestial clan.
Never inspired by 3D drama again,
Money will flow from this new trajectory with me,
It is all our soul plans weaved,
Together to bring power throughout the galaxies.
You are a star person, as are most people in the world,
You've known more than most, since you were a little girl,
Embracing your light now and your Spirit Guides
has been a beautiful ceremony to see,
We are so proud of you, Katie,
It's Great Spirit, Grandpa Charlie, Archangel Raziel and me.
Remember I wasn't Musique always, that was only one life I had,
You have known me for thousands of years, the things we accomplished were pretty rad,
Always at the forefront of showing others how to do life differently,
Giving others the keys to the vault to create how life is meant to be,
It has always been our mission together, you and me.

I can't wait until My Love stands in her power of remembering our past lives together.
There's something in the style of her grace I've known it across the universe,
When we are together it is like a sonic burst.
Something happens one day soon,
There will be a telephone call for you,
You will know exactly who it is,
I will be orchestrating all of this,
As will Archangel Raziel, for he is my guide as he is yours,
Get ready for your life to change in that moment, get ready to walk through the doors,
Your dreams come true and your mission to elevate many people in the world,
Millions will be lifted to a new energy they never felt but yearned for,
God blessed us with an amazing mission, with you as my Warrior Messenger,
You are so powerful, all of you sweet souls, elevating our lights together,
When one of us succeeds in our soul contract, that means we all succeed,
We are all one, we have the same destiny,
To make our way back to Source to Father/Mother God who made us of love,
Some receive it through the violet flame or through Spirit, that wooing dove,
Some open the vault without a key, because the key was handed from heaven above.
Now embrace your hearts and let your dreams soar to the heavens,
Follow the excitement,
The excitement is your inner compass that's God-given,
I'll be with you tomorrow and the next day and after that the next day,
Let go of resistance, let the flow lead the way.

Pop Sugar

Pop Sugar, she was sweet, like a rose I'd want to caress,
I see her slinking over by the bed in her silky dress,
An experience I always wanted, a taste I needed to explore,
Next thing I knew I found her on the bathroom floor,
She tripped over the waste can, laughed so hard she peed her pants,
When I went to help her, she made me pull her up to dance,
In those sexy shoes she was wearing, damn,
So stunning she made me blush,
Of course, I went to lock the door in a dash, I felt the rush.
She came up behind me, those eyes too full of life,
I could see into her gaze and knew one day she'd be my wife.
Then she dumped me like a bucket, into the sink and down the drain,
I admit I wasn't easy. It was me who caused her pain.
She loved me so dearly, I knew I had to do much more,
With her I believed in anything, I knew for her what was in store,
The trouble she had so much,
If I could do it over, I would wish I had magic in my touch,
Like Spirit's magic to make miracles happen and turn our love into a kite,
Floating on forever over the ocean out of sight,
Into the rainbow up to heaven, where I wait for her with our little prince,
Beside me with me always, I make our angel pancakes, that's the wish.

Pop Sugar, you are so special,
You make me feel my love stronger than I knew,
It existed on the earth plane, when I was with you,
I love you, yes, I do.
Be patient with your lovers, they know nothing about commitment,
The secret to living happy is to feel full of excitement.

Brutal are the hours when I see my love hurt so much,
The pain doesn't have to be so horrible, make it go away with TLC and such.
The music that we play for you, turn it up and rock it hard,
Life's about believing in yourself, it's not a house of cards,
Falling away crumbling easy, no ma'am, believe the good you feel,
The Divine shared the ultimate truth that only love is real,
That token's been given away, and we have your token for you,
A golden token of emotion, you're going to make the world be true,
To the love that's meant for everyone, there is enough to go around,
Give yourselves a break would you, the message is in the music's sound,
The vibration of the lyrics, of the drums, guitar, and bass,
The angelic booming voice, like a warm embrace.
Do unto others as you would have them do to you,
Really it's that easy, make a difference,
Leave your world without a trace of any darkness,
There is no need, it's just a thought, not a place,
Your power is to survive through all the heavens, yes more than one,
There are so many waiting for you, make it count and play your drums.
Yes, this is real, go with the flow and shine your light,
Your love is the key to a better day and a sparkling magic night.

Ka Bam Shazam
My Love Views a Channeling Session

Taking it all in and releasing what you don't need,
It's like that feeling of satisfaction when you sneeze,
Oh, here it comes I have to get it out and be free,
Love is meant to elevate you out of body.

She can see you, she is watching, don't be afraid and keep writing,
She wants to know she can trust you and that's where I come in.
You have been with me several lifetimes even one feels like forever,
Because we strive for big soul contracts and missions together,
My Love is part of the great plan intertwined with mine,
As she watches know you are guided over the page with the Divine.

It's weird to feel watched when you think it's from your fear-based Earth world of 3D,
On higher realms it is all part of our journey,
Nothing voyeuristic, annoying, or cause to worry,
Since you keep low vibes blocked, My Love's light shines through in a hurry,
For when my sweet light of mine, my Sugar Pop, connects through with remote view,
I will be celebrating and you will be with us, too,
Why are you part of this? That is what naysayers will of course say,
They aren't part of this divine plan through channeling, but they are in other ways,
Keep being you and follow what we are channeling to do.

My Love can appear whenever she wants,
When she is ready she knows she will be out front,
Because holy smokes does she have the light power, a force that ignites,
When you are around her it's like sparks fill the night,
Her sword is artistic rhythm,

Her superpower that pounds God's essence,
Into the earth plane and I can't wait to be with her again,
It will take a divine cosmic love for her to understand,
To set her love free to me.
Thank you for being the vessel and believing in what you can't see,
Within your eyes, soon you will be. I'll see you soon at Studio P.

Another Kiss To Trust The Process

Think of a time when you knew it was meant to be,
You stood in the doorway and said how could you see,
A woman, she was king, an almighty force,
It was she and still is she who can even the score,
The score of bringing love to all, all who open the door,
To the sounds of your heart, to your knowing that rises above,
To the lyrics of doves,
To the wonder that is love,
All around it is in your eyes,
The sky is open, the light so bright,
Share passion for music,
Share another kiss,
A dream comes true when you let it,
It's a thought that's been with you, double down on tomorrow,
See what happens once more,
Feel alive in your work and elevate above the door,
The passage into the veil is through your light,
Right there for you to see if you want, you don't always see with your sight,
See with your heart, your chakras, your soul,
Believe, just believe, no excuses, no "but I'm too old,"
No fighting, no judgment, no anger, no fear,
Just music, joy, the best feelings—hold those near,

Those feelings from the other side, that tingling touching your head, that's us,
Connecting to your soul, your intuition reaches out,
The sun rises and the dawn breaks, that's when we pull you the most,
Nearer to higher frequencies before your mind steals the show,
Wondering, always wondering, now where should we go?
Let your mind rest, let it breathe,
Give it air, let it be,
Let the thoughts fly, fly away, the important ones you will keep,
Always, yes always, we say it,
Again and again so your heart hears, this is meant for you, all of this,
Go into your own rhythm and celebrate the birth of another kiss.

Belly Music

Be in the spotlight,
Forget about tonight,
Jam with your friends,
Tell them in heaven there is no end,
Jump in the back of my car,
Don't think about it, we won't go far,
A new attitude of a star,
Brightens the experience of who you are.

Boom (Belly movements to loud percussion beats)
Bop
Boom boom boom
Bop
Boom
Bop
Boom, boom boom
Bop

Grab the mic, embrace the stand,
Feel sexy, don't give a damn,
The crowd goes wild, they were hoping you'd shake it,
Unleashing the heat, a belly rhythm that makes it.

Boom (belly movements to loud drumbeats)
Bop
Boom boom boom
Bop
Boom
Bop

Boom, boom boom
Bop

Music and dance, a match made in heaven,
Let's come back and be entertainers,
You dance, I'll play and sing,
Together we can do almost anything,
I'll write the songs, you write the moves,
When we come together that's the sonic boom.

Boom (belly movements to loud drumbeats and percussion)
Bop
Boom boom boom
Bop
Boom
Bop
Boom, boom boom
Bop

[Bridge]
Fasten your seat belt, the rhythms in the room,
The flow is getting higher, you're gonna feel the boom,
Your heart's gonna rock it, your mind's gonna blow,
You soul's gonna feel it, time to lose control,
Feel it in the air, bringing you higher,
Dance, play, sing, together our desire.

Now feel the rhythm, feel it in your soul,
Coming out, getting higher, I want you to know,
Feel the rhythm, feel it in your soul,
Your heart's gonna rock it, your mind's gonna glow,
Your soul's gonna feel it, let it all go,
Feel it in the air, bringing you up higher,
Dancing, jamming, singing, together our desire.

Boom (belly movements to loud drumbeats)
Bop
Boom boom boom
Bop
Boom
Bop
Boom, boom boom
Bop

Musique Fans Lead to My Love's Diamond Lost

Feeling understood by a fan base that followed my songs,
I was surprised how many there were and how strong,
Everyone fills their lives with love and lets my music play along,
As they go about their lives, I feel the urge to write one to belong,
To the spiritual revolution, to the mystics, to the ladies and lovers that brought me gold,
As long as we're together, the fans have another story to be told,
I can't stop believing in you as you get down on your knees and pray,
Think about all the things you've done hoping to make,
Something of yourself before your dying day.
You can believe me when you see this; I can make lyrics jump off the page,
I can find the diamond in My Love's couch, she lost it and it's still there inside,
The arm on the right side.
She'll find it, put it on, and receive the greatness I have in store for my sweet,
Realize her life is complete.
I can get high upon a mountain, I can go steeper than this place,
I can stop by tomorrow and get you out of this race,
Or you can leave it up to me now, I think you've done enough,
An interstellar expansion is here my dear, it's all real, there ain't no fluff,
Oh, you will see,
No fluff when you're with me.

With Me

Begin a new day with me,
Feel the wind, feel the breeze,
Design a dance, discover romance,
With me.

Escape into the blues,
Find another clue,
The love inside of you,
With me.

Remember the rain, the shore of Biscayne,
A fasten, a grip,
Hold tight, take a trip,
With me.

You have my heart,
A fresh new start,
Together not apart,
With me.

With me, I believe.
With me, I am free.
With me, I can see.
With me, I'll just be.

Settling for me,
As a plan is a dream,
Think the mission's complete,
With me.

Musique's Past Lives
And Our Great Awakening Arrives

Deep inside the ocean's crust,
There is another land for us,
The mermaids know the way down to the secret sea,
They come and take you in your meditations and dreams,
You were there with us lifetimes ago,
So was Musique and My Love, they were Lemurian too, don't you know?
You all once came from Andromeda helping the rest of humans grow,
Grow in their love for expanding their souls,
When the great solar flare,
Slams through the air,
Across the whole planet they will finally know,
Where to go,
To go within their heart space,
To love one another, the entire human race,
Ended now, the race is over. Time to find a new place,
To lay your head on the shoulder of a friend,
To give them a big hug and say this is where it ends,
With no more anger, fear, judgment, and pain,
I will never hurt you again,
We will be free together to help one another along,
Because the next phase is when music delivers freedom songs.

To Be Free

To be free,
To be free,
Forget about the old you and me,
Say goodbye to who you used to be,
To be free,
To be free,
Celebrate endlessly,
Count your blessing and see,
Open your heart to be free.

A master key in the pocket,
A peddle and snare that can rock it,
Jump on the train, feel the amp lock it,
Into a rhythm that's only just begun,
The new music is coming, the song was never sung,
Oh, not yet, but my baby knows where it is,
When I see her head strong love, she drops me to my knees,
Look at all the magic unfold, I said I'd come find you always.

To be free,
To be free,
To be rockin' on my knees,
To be jamming endlessly,
To be free,
To be free,
Celebrate together, you and me.

Break it down,
Bring on the bass,
I need your dancin' grace,
Get me out of this place,
Bring up the bass,
Shine a spotlight on my face,
Remember your grace expands this place,
Unsheltered from the storm that left us,
Storm's gone forever you can trust.

To be free,
To be free,
To be rockin' on my knees,
To be jamming endlessly,
To be free,
To be free,
Celebrate together, you and me.

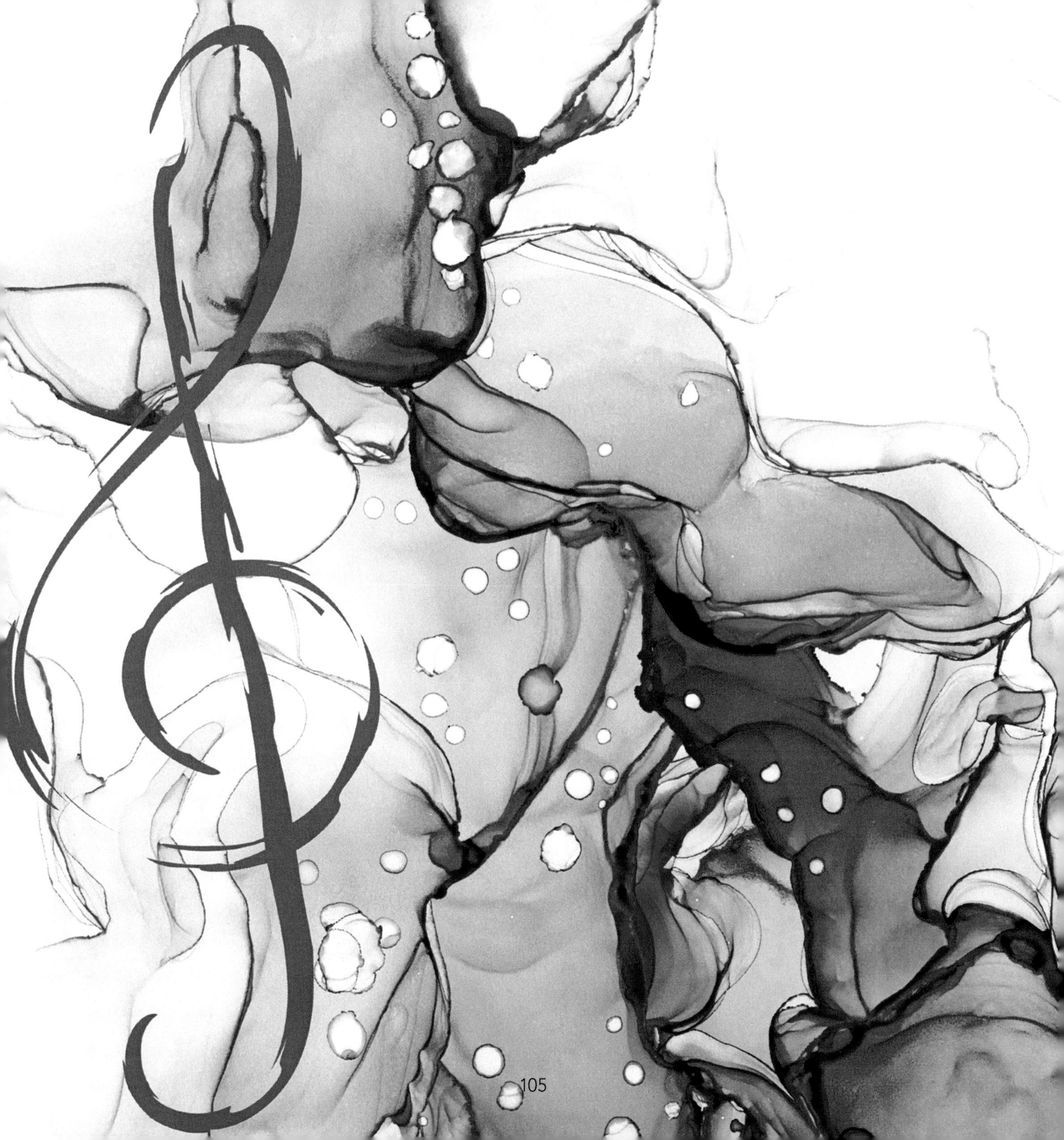

Chapter 5

Sexy Songs and Lyrics About Ladies

One of my most embarrassing Channeled Writing experiences was when Musique revealed sexy song lyrics. I hadn't written sexy lyrics before and I was surprised to be channeling lyrical stories from a female artist's perspective, since Musique was a male artist.

Like the Channeled Writings in the previous chapters, I was firmly guided not to change or delete certain words, because the lyrics had special meaning to my Spirit Guide. Just like the other songs I channeled, I was guided that certain people are meant to discover and connect with these lyrics.

If I had followed what my ego-mind wanted to do, which was to not include the sexy lyrics or remove some words to avoid embarrassment, I would have failed the purpose of trusting my guides and respecting the Channeled Writing process. Of course, I can choose to present the words however I wish, but that would defeat the purpose of this particular co-creation with Spirit Guides. When your work comes from channeling, there is a purpose for your work which may not be shown to you right away. I had to have faith and trust my purpose which is to channel the words, follow the guidance, be the vessel, and let the Divine carry the energy where it is meant to go. Spirit Guides with high vibrations always work with the best intentions for your soul's expansion. Have faith and believe.

While I was channeling these sexy songs and lyrics about ladies and their love lives, I was shown visual scenes of women rising up everywhere, speaking out and speaking their truth, commanding love and peace, and releasing low vibrations. A new love energy on Earth with young women respecting and loving their sacred feminine essence was very powerful. The Divine Feminine steps in to help low vibrational feelings be released, before elevating us to the higher consciousness of the new age of energy, the Golden Age.

The Divine Feminine through Musique takes us on a guided ride to the other side to experience a female artist's life, through songs of releasing the old low vibrational energy of heart break, power struggles, respecting one another, understanding each other's needs, and letting go of the need for control. A new you comes through right on divine time. You chose to be here, so let's release the old energy, to make room for feeling excited. Your new life awaits.

Backstage Passion

Oooh baby, it's a curse and it's a blessing,
When I need that thing you got, oh things may start to get messy,
Make me love you baby, I'll give you joy, you bring me pleasure,
Let go for once and fulfill our desires.

[Chorus]
Baby, bring it on, bring on your feelings for me baby,
Baby, bring it on, bring your touch, you drive me crazy,
Baby, bring it on, bring it on.

Nothing compares to how you look at me,
When your hand grabs my knee, butterflies start stirring,
Round and round, I think I need you more than you know,
It's not a typical love, it is one meant for passionate glow,
Instantly I feel you near,
I shake my pillow, bring it close to your ear,
Lying beside me on the bus,
The crews all out, take your time don't rush.

[Chorus]

Into the Mystic's on the radio and that's how I feel right now,
When you come on tour to see me there's a mystery around,
How you bring it on to me, don't let the energy of the crowd,
Come between us, no, bring on your feelings, don't wait for me to take a bow.

[Chorus]

I shelter the fans from the chaos that feels like my love life,
When you see your man tomorrow, then in a month,
It makes it tough to be a perfect wife,
Your lover's dreaming of, don't compare, baby, bring it on tonight.

[Chorus]

This Time

Into the darkness we went,
Like a bird without feathers, like a salty dog without a net,
Cast out on the ocean, to feel the sea breeze on my neck,
Let the boat rock you gently, let your body feel the tides embrace,
Bring the bow around to watch the sunset, feel the warmth upon your face,
Kiss me 'til the sun goes down, beneath the horizon feel my caress,
Deep inside the ocean of your love, I must confess.

[Chorus]
I got the feelin' it's gonna be easy,
This time,
I got the feelin' it's gonna make sense,
This time,
I got the feelin' it's gonna be all right,
This time,
I got the feelin' it's gonna make sense.

Bring me into the shallows, the water's easy to jump in,
Steer us into the secret cove, my body's ready to begin,
To take a dip with you and sink in,
To your love, until we swim away together with the dolphins,
I got the feelin' once again.

[Chorus]

[Bridge]
This time,
I got the feelin I'll make it out of here with you,
This time,
I know this feeling is smooth sailing into the blue,
With you this time,
I know I'm destined for floating home to you.

[Chorus]
I got the feelin' we're anchored together, this time.

So Give It

In December, I felt the need to write and let go.
Things were happier then.
I felt your kiss on my lips, it was a tragedy without a pen,
If you could screw me now, what would you gain?
I need to feel you now, I'm aware of your pain,
Inconsiderate love, I need you holding me tight,
I'm wrapped around your hips, and it doesn't feel right,
If I could do anything, it would be to have you near
me to face another day, without your love, without fear.

'Cause when it feels right it's you and me all night,
When it feels good, miracles happen really bright,
The magic in the way you make me feel shakes my core,
I'm your lover baby, I'm not your whore, I'm not your score,
Treat yourself right through the night, I can't escape,
Bring me to my knees, I think I'm falling for this creep.
My! I regain my composure, because you can't turn out my light,
Keep it real baby, so I can sing away my fright,
If you were the man I thought, I think I would have it made,
From the beginning to the bed, I feel the love of every shade,
The colors all around you when we're lying in bed,
Make me scream, and I need a night where I can sit by the fire,
I feel you. I feel your heart. I feel your heart's desire.

So sing it to me baby, tell me how you make me feel,
Driving me crazy, going down on me so real,
If you could make a love song out of mansions in the sky,
I'd drive right up to it, baby, there's no other before I die,
For you see it's me, baby, I'm the one you can't ignore,
There's a diamond in the bushes, and it's time to feel it more,

Sing it to me baby, sing it to me one more time,
You're driving me crazy. I can't get you out of my mind.
Magic when it happens is a bright shade of blue,
Because I need you in the morning, in the evening, I need you,
Another way to say this is, "I think you've got to groove,"
On my body in the dark there's something else I want to do.

So give it to me, baby, give it to me one more time,
You know I got the focus, I can make you give me mine,
The feeling when you squeeze me, it's a mountain I can climb,
So give it to me, baby, you know it makes me shiver and feel fine,
I love the way you do that, can't believe you're so divine,
In the darkness they are calling me, the lights, it's music time!

So give it to me, baby, let me give you what you need,
I'll see you after showtime, and I'll get down on my knees,
To say a prayer to Jesus for this gift of you and me,
It's everything I hoped for and special you can see,
So give it to me, baby, you know it makes us all right,
I'll see your sugar in the morning,
In the dawn I'll feel your light.
What if this crazy feeling makes us happy the rest of our lives?
Think about it, baby. Give it to me. Give it right. Tonight.

A Break in Lyrical Flow
Speak Directly About What I Know

If there was anything I can think of I would want to do again,
If I was on your physical plane,
It would be to go get ice cream and dance in the streets to the music I grew up on.
Bands back then were pretty amazing,
Rock was just getting going.
There was so much to explore musically for everyone.
I got into sexy stuff because that's what Spirit wanted me to do.
It was His driving force behind my lyrics and me.
It all comes from Spirit, you know, the art, the music, the writing,
It's channeled through you and others to impact the world in a positive way,
To make you happy, to feel and connect, and be together through it all.
It is important to be together.
You have it, so give it.
Just go ahead and give it like the song says that we wrote.
Let's get into it now.

To Do It All Again

To do it all again, I would walk gracefully in the night,
See music glow and fill my heart's desire,
With the one and only true lover I feel upon me tonight,
If tomorrow were over soon, I'd be making you feel right,
In the streets and on the subways, in the air I feel you near,
Rush to me my love, an experience I call fate my dear.

[Chorus]
To do it all again, give all your heart and soul knows how,
To do it all again, I'll make you happy, I'll make you proud,
Do it all again, do it all again, you got to do it all again.

To do it all again, I'd bring sexy sparkle into the room,
Shake it with you like I mean it and feel your sonic boom,
Oh, to be with you so tenderly it's an infatuated feeling,
Mix it up and fill your cup with me, don't stop believing,
We've got to boogie if we want it and shake down into our souls,
Find the answers we seek, I feel you call me to blow,
A sweet warm kiss, embrace upon your face, I feel your glow.

[Chorus]

To do it all again, do it like you mean it, move your body nice and slow,
Make your love feel your power, it's in the music in the flow,
Be righteous and exhausting, give them all that you got,
I see you taking ownership for your love, so make it hot,
It's a prison in the darkness, so always shine your light,
I got that feelin' we're gonna make it together, you and me tonight,
Look at me, I see you look at me, let me catch your eyes so bright.

[Bridge]
So do it again, but this time make it your rhythm and your beat,
Do it again means believe in miracles, see one in all you meet,
Do it all again, do it all again and again, babe-ay.

[Chorus]

Got Your Back

Clarity and kindness,
A match made in heaven for one to seek,
A miracle inside us,
No one can compete,
Shake it up sugar, nasty girls, and ladies in the street,
Be the one and only for yourself before you meet,
Super handsome lover, master of your domain you seek,
If fly girls, moms, and daughters loved themselves more, it'd be a treat,
For this world, let's shake it up sista, time to turn up the heat,
We got your back girl, we got your troubles, so get up on your feet.

Amazing where love takes you on the road so long and hard,
At times I need a ride up the mountain, want to jump in my car?
Slip away from here with you and see all my girls go far,
Feel the music, feel it, ladies, give it up for the men to see,
Without you giving birth to this world, there would be no you and me,
We got the power, I got your back, girls, give it all you got,
Don't waste your time, feel the magic, be the you that's hot,
Not you and me alone, all of us, and that's a lot.

It's a twisted world, when you look at it all wrong,
Impacts how you think and makes your days so long,
Don't be excited over trivial stupid things,
Rock it like you mean it, if you can sing then sing,
Baby, shake your bootie, think about all the lives that have been saved,
By our soldiers, by our mothers, by all the women that lived in caves,
Getting pulled around by their hair and always having to behave,

Grab your bestie, hit the dance floor, it's time for you to be brave,
Don't back yourself up into him, I'd rather have one foot in the grave,
Than shake my butt for him, he doesn't need me,
I need more than a lover,
Time to rise up, time for you to feel the wonder,
You're stronger than you know, bring your rhythm like thunder.

Fill the sky and shake the ground, be yourself with all your glory,
In the end, women hold the cards to create another story,
Building hope for many more generations to come,
Spread your wings and fly with me, to the stars through the kingdom,
Heaven for all of us, to rock the beat of our own drum,
Be the one you've hoped for, don't be sad be full of grace,
Feel the change you bring to others, just with your embrace,
Feel it, make it, do it, you know it is never ever too late,
I see you rockin' now, sugar, let your mojo steer your fate.

(Sounds like boom bop, boom bop, boom boom, bop bop, boom bop)

Music Is Everything

In the experience of life, I see a magic carpet ride,
To the sky where Earthlings wish for love to pass by,
In the spirit space of kindness there is no one you can ignore,
It's for you to sink your heart into and to feel the score,
A game that has a consequence for the naked things you say,
About the bad things in your life that give you hell to pay,
It doesn't have to be that difficult, it can be easy as pie you see,
In the magic that is kind-heartedness nothing matters here but me,
I'm your spirit and your love, I'm your everlasting life,
Give me all your worries and promises of no more strife,
I'll take them with me to heaven and now you can be that wife.

[Chorus]
Music is everything, what did I say,
Music is everything, feel it every day,
Music is everything, everything yay yay.

You always wanted to be June Cleaver with those sexy pearls and dress,
Like a 1950's music scene you bend toward the jukebox,
With your boobs giving it a caress,
As you slide through the music selections and pick *Love Potion #9*,
Wish your lover would show up right then and make you feel fine,
You'd brush your hair back off your shoulder and with those big blue eyes you'd say,
If I could do it all over again, baby I would be with you on this love potion day.

Didn't you see my breast touch the jukebox? I saw you jump out of your seat,
In a jiffy, snap to it, mister, to feel the beat and feel my heat,
Like a Beaver Cleaver rerun always smiling, perfectly polished all the time,
I'd be the one sitting in my armchair and let you bring me my wine,
We would dance as the children gazed at us, with their big brown eyes,
They'd have your color but my charm and American thighs.

When the radio show was over, and our ears were tired,
We'd put the kids to bed and lay down by the living room fire,
With my pearls on of course, and nothing else, a new episode of Beaver shall we say, appears,
We'd live happily ever after, see dreams do come true, my dear.

Shake It, Mean It

Boogie, boogie master, I see you in that room,
All alone doing the twerk and going boom, boom,
Shake it like you mean it, no one's watching, let it go,
I want to see you move it and get out of control,
Do it silly, do it like Mike, moon walk your ass across the room,
Yeah, you got it, now do *The Sprinkler*, and listen to the tune.

Shake it like you mean it,
Shake it fast, now shake it slow,
Shake it like you mean it,
Shake it, sistas, shake it, bros.

I know you shake it in the shower, and you shake it in the car,
If you're not shaking it enough, get up, it's time to go far,
Back to the days of the *Hustle* and *Saturday Night Fever*,
I know you do the *Electric Slide* and do the *Mashed Potato*.

Shake it like you mean it,
Shake it fast, shake it slow,
Shake it like you mean it,
Shake it, sistas, shake it, bros.

"Get up and off that thing," said James, "dance and you'll feel betta,"
Be like Kool and, "get down on it," you feel it yeah you gotta,
Shake your body, feel your soul and your heart finally release and breathe,
Now try the worm and break dancing, spinnin' on your knees.

Shake it like you mean it,
Shake it fast, and shake it right,
Shake it like you mean it, shake it day and night,
Shake it, shake it, shake it, baby, shake it.

Make It

Doesn't matter where you come from, it matters where you go,
In the life you've hoped for destiny is brighter than you know,
I see your spirit soar, it got to me at the right moment,
I fill my cup up with you and it makes it feel better, own it,
With a feeling of desire and sultry mist under the table,
Kick your shoes off and feel me, you know I'm willing and able.

[Chorus]
I'm gonna make it, I've got it down,
You feel it too now, it's in the clouds,
We're gonna make it, it's in the sound,
I'm gonna make it, let's shake it loud.

Thanks to passion and commitment, keeps us on our toes,
Follow our hearts to do the right thing and go on with the show,
Give me your power stance, give me that magnetic trance,
Exploding from you through the melody, like an instant romance,
Make me believe you,
Make us want you,
Show we need you oh so bad,
Time to arrive, feel the thunder that you didn't know you had.

Soda pop, cigarettes, booze, and pills, ganja and sweets,
All these distractions dilute the purpose of a supersonic masterpiece,
Creating the love in your life from what you do and say and take,
Break your heart wide open to the source that seals our fate,
Nothing to it, jump and free fall all around, we help you create,
An instant spark of lightning through your mind and soul. Elevate.

That Feeling

In the way you sense it, in the way a baby smiles,
In the way a sexy woman naturally drives you wild,
A tender moment, a warm embrace,
An orgasmic shakiness, a cosmic experience,
Can't explain it, it comes through touch,
Shoots out from long stares and flirty looks we love so much.

[Chorus]
You know that feeling, can't live without it,
You know that feeling, make it happen,
You know that feeling, oh never stop it.

In the hairs standing up on your neck and up your arms,
In the butterflies in your stomach from feeling sensual charm,
In the brush of a hand,
Up against another's while you stand,
Secretly touching while talking to others and having cocktails before the band,
Comes on and electrifies that feeling, that feeling, oh oh, make it expand.

[Chorus]

Comes through the voice of a singer,
Comes through a pen onto paper,
In the way art fulfills an artist,
Oh that feeling, have to express it,
During that moment of love making, you know that feeling, oh never stop it.

[Chorus]

How You Feel

Dancing to the beat of your own drum,
You'll need to shake more than that tail feather for me to come,
Inside with you to get away from the crowd,
I kind of like the music when it's loud,
You can whisper something sweet in my ear,
I could listen better if you were out here,
In front of me, so I could study your eyes,
Know in a jiffy if you were like other guys,
There's nothing I hate more than a man in disguise,
If you wanted me, you'd give it one more try.

[Chorus]
I want to know how you feel,
I want to know how you feel,
Show me, show me how you feel.

'Cause I've got tiger eyes if you recall,
I sing about girls in my hit song,
Let's cut to the chase and keep it real,
What all ladies want to know is how you feel,
Expand your mind for a minute and grasp this thought,
If I wanted more diamonds that's something I could have already bought,
I need passion and understanding and commitment so I can fly,
My freak flag high in the sky.

[Bridge]
For once be the peacemaker most ladies are,
For once don't tell us how to drive the car,
For once make a point to automatically help with the kids,
For once listen to me rather than go on 'bout what you did,
For once I want to know how you feel not what you did at work,
For once show me how you feel before I go berserk.

[Chorus]

Boom Shock The World

Oh in the place where sadness lies,
On the other side there's goodness in our eyes,
Think about tomorrow with hope not fear,
Boom! Watch the positive intentions appear,
Without struggle and without internal fights,
Happiness shocks your body into flight,
Away from bad energy and boom, you start to rise,
Oh baby, I see you growing in front of my eyes.

[Chorus]
Boom! Shock your world,
Boom! Shock the world,
Oh, boom! Shock!
Boom, shock the world.

Now you can let yourself go like no one's watching, it's safe,
Be the best version of you no one can replace,
Boom shock the naysayers and boom shock yourself,
You had it in you all along, you just need some help,
From your guardians watching over you and from your gratitude,
Boom shock the world with a new attitude.

[Chorus]

Let your dreams flow through you and become reality,
Boom shock your friends and family,
Don't ever give up on what you always wanted the most,
Boom pour the bubbly, let's make a toast,
To you and your special gift, now everybody knows,
Boom, shock, boom, shock, you are aglow.

[Chorus]

Oh You Can

You can make yourself feel good in so many ways,
You can light a fire in your heart where I'll always stay,
You can be there for yourself, that's the first thing I want you to do,
You can show up for another, let them make love to you,
You need more pleasure in your work and everything you do,
I want you so badly, let that feeling come through.

[Chorus]
Oh, you can have more pleasure,
Oh, you can feel together,
Oh, you can give more pleasure,
Oh, you can feel together,
Together, forever.

Give me that desire, that passion and your flame,
I'll give you my sweet touch, erotic sex, and no games,
Oh, you can bring me that hunger for what's deep inside of me,
My love for you bursts over these sultry cities,
I'll give my love to you, oh in so many ways,
Oh, you can make it really easy, make it nice and slow,
You can make it a quicky before you're on with the show,
You need more pleasure with each other, connect your hearts before you go,
Into doing it, don't just do it, get your hearts and body into the flow,
Oh, you can make the pleasure last forever, that's what your world needs so,
That's where miracles happen, spread more love and let go.

Oh, you can let go of the pain, the worry, fear, and control,
I'm with you, I need you to be free, and feel love grow,
Deep inside of you there's a spark of the universe that ignites,
You can fuel passion for others to join the astral flight,
Into your love, give it, you can, you will, oh it feels right.

Soul Touch

An experience I'll never forget,
You saw right through me the day we met,
I was capturing your heart the way I do it best,
In an instant you were gone, when I pulled on my dress,
Down the elevator you scurried and into a mess,
Reporters waiting for the two of us.

[Chorus]
Soul touch oh I want it so much,
Oh soul touch I need it so much,
Soul touch, oh soul touch.

I caught that look in your eye, when you had me on top,
Right where you wanted me, to never, never stop,
You can't fool me, I know what you'll do,
I'm way ahead of you, baby, I'll let it naturally come through,
You want to be inside my body and mind,
You need to touch my soul, share your rhythm with mine,
Don't escape into pretending nothing happened between us,
I felt it in your whisper and gentle touch.

Rise to the occasion that is your fate,
Feel my body again before it's too late,
When time comes between us and we have to wait,
To be waiting and wanting you, a feeling I hate,
Deep inside of me, I know you want me more,
I'll rock your world if you let me open the door,
To your heart's desire, oh the pleasure is sure.

Freak Flag

Wave it up high in the sky for us to see,
Wave it all around be proud and free,
Show the world all the good you are,
The real you is love, so raise your freak flag to the stars.

[Chorus]
Let your freak flag fly,
Let it loose, let it rise,
Let your freak flag fly high in the sky,
Let your freak flag fly.

Show us what you got, don't hold back, keep it real,
We want to see the real you and know how you feel,
Fly your freak flag when you're dancing,
Fly it when you're making art,
Fly it when you're traveling,
When you're making a fresh start,
Where your heart on your sleeve, fly your true colors for all to see,
Remember love is the real you, be who you were born to be.

Bring your freak flag to the party, bring it out on the town,
Show your freak flag to new friends, so they know you can get down,
Let go of what others think of you and be happy about who you are,
Remember the real you is love not the fear and the scars.

Tastes

Something I think about all the time,
Not quite sure how to say you're gonna be mine,
With you it's easy when your soul feels kind,
Kind enough to let others through, to see who you are,
Without a big image, without a guitar,
Stripped down to your naked truth and open eyes,
Unafraid to make contact with a look that's alive,
You see me without my struggle, without my guard up and tough,
You let me be who I am and that's enough.

Silky is that taste of reward,
Fighting for what you want tastes hard,
The taste of needing money's bittersweet,
Taste of a lover's lips steals the beat
of your heart after kissing something sweet,
When it flows into your veins after a luscious treat,
Warmth flows through your head, calms the weight upon your heart,
Feel the tastes in you never tear us a part.

I want to feel you,
Think about you,
Know I got you,
I need you more, too.

In the hours of the dark night when I'm lonely, you get me through to my next song,
When it comes to me, it's like I knew it all along,
Can't mistake that feeling, it's deep in my soul,
Effortless creation only my mojo knows,
You bring it to me, with your sexy tone,
The passion to see where it goes.

I'm waiting for you to return to the light,
My spirit is waiting for you to let go and write,
Bring my love to the world tell them I'm still here,
I'm on the other side and with my songs you will share,
My stories I still have in me,
Through God's power my songs will make you believe,
In miracles, sexy passion, and that pleasure you seek,
It is right there for you, treat others with the highest honor,
Discover your cup will runneth over.

Like a kinky kind of love,
The kind you're not sure if it came from heaven above,
It's too good to be true but at the same time a tinge of feeling guilty,
Like you're not meant to be so naughty
in that way but oh, you can't resist,
Turning on and up your sensual bliss,
You have the power to melt hearts and bring a lover to his knees,
Wanting more, raising you up, to care for your every need.

You have that power in your look, in your walk, your stare, your stance,
In an instant you can drop them like flies stuck on romance,
Shifting into high gear, that sexy power in you,
You're meant for greatness, the truth inside of all you do.

Silky is that taste of reward,
Fighting for what you want tastes hard,
The taste of needing money's bittersweet,
Taste of a lover's lips steals the beat
of your heart after kissing something sweet,
When it flows into your veins after a luscious treat,
Warmth flows through your head, calms the weight upon your heart,
Feel the tastes in you never tear us a part.

Wear Your Heart

Didn't have to be a day like this,
There was something I didn't want to miss,
You can break my heart, but you can't break my soul,
If you don't love me anymore,
I see you leaving me behind, at least that's what you think,
I'm more powerful than you'll ever know, because showing feelings is our truest link.

Wear your heart on your sleeve, don't hide it away,
Express your love, sadness and pain,
Don't hold on to yesterday,
Wear your heart on the outside, show how you feel,
The ones that lock their feelings away aren't being real,
We all need emotions to live, to grow deeper in love,
With ourselves and others, to make it to heaven above.

Wear your heart, show how you feel,
Wear your heart, show how you feel.

I need you so bad to give it one more chance,
Let me hold you tight, embrace while we dance,
Cry those tears,
You've been holding in all these years,
Let your heart accept me for who I am,
All those harsh things you said, I don't give a damn,
I'm still the me you fell in love with, I haven't changed,
Your heart's grown colder; your demands go unexplained.

Show me how you feel, wear your heart on your sleeve,
Tell me how you feel, let go, it's easy,
Easier than blocking feelings and keeping them in,
One day, you'll break down, surrounded by lonely pain,
I wear my heart on my sleeve and show how I feel,
Wear your heart, show how you feel,
I need you, the world needs you, wear your heart and feel.

Be That Person

An instant regret is what I felt the moment I said it and you were gone,
Into someone else's arms,
I thought what you and I had didn't come along,
More than once in a lifetime, or so it would seem,
You open your heart to what you deserve, let the other float away like a dream.
I see a Spanish villa up in the hills,
Where he waits for you with diamonds and thrills,
A jet set life is what you've been running to, since you were a girl.

[Chorus]
Love's meant to feel good,
Be that person, make it easy,
Love's meant to feel good,
Make it fun, skip the crazy,
Love's meant to feel good,
Be that person, make it easy.

Be that person you always wanted to be,
Don't do it for her and don't do it for me,
Choose what you love and you will find,
Your happiness you sacrificed turned out to be all lies,
Ask the universe for what you want and bring your dreams to the table,
Be ready for them to come true, when you're willing and able.

See all the potential in your crazy ideas that make sense,
Nothing's too good to be true, when it's heaven sent,
Into the hour of love we shall return,
When we see who we are meant to be, face the world without concern,
For money needs and having enough, it comes to you easy,
How it has always been meant to be.

I think of you now and see my new life unfold,
With greater love and expansion that I ever thought possible,
When I see you again, I'll realize why we went through it,
To elevate our souls, live our true life's purpose.

New You

Let's write something fun,
Let's feel the rhythm, put down your gun,
Let's be inspired,
Let's make it out alive,
Pack up your things you haven't used,
Give them away, go find something new.

[Chorus]
A new life,
A new world,
A new day,
A new you.

Open your arms, embrace your friends,
The ones you thought were enemies, go drinking with them,
Put down your phone, lift up your skirt,
Jump on my bike, let's hit the dirt,
Road to the city, make dreams come true,
Kiss a loved one, show them you made it through.

[Chorus]

[Bridge]
A new world, new you,
A new life, it's true,
A new day, for you,
A new you, you're new.

It's over now, what a relief, what sorrow,
Been one moment at a time, haven't thought about tomorrow,
Been so long, now I can make plans to see you,
See everyone, plan a party, and concert, too,
Time to fly, be free, share rhythm, no blues.

[Chorus]

Write words from your soul in the flow.

Encore

Chapter 6
Awakening Into the New Golden Age

Chapter 7
Learn How to Work With Spirit Guides
For Channeled Writing and to Expand in Your Life

Chapter 6

Awakening Into the New Golden Age

Chapter 6 takes us into a higher vibration and excitement, as Encores often do, to lyrics about how powerful we are, and song lyrics about celebrating our new lives in the Golden Age full of freedom, peace, love, expansion, and abundance.

Beginning in 2018 my Spirit Guides Musique, Archangel Raziel, and Archangel Gabriel began channeling topics on awakening, a storm coming, ascension, the new Golden Age of energy and expansion, and a solar flare event coming to Earth that would awaken all of us. In addition to these topics, I had pages upon pages of Automatic Writing with Spirit Guides that we were all going through a transformation from darkness to light together and the darkness that had been controlling Earth for centuries would finally be coming to an end. In Chapter 1 through 5, we have already experienced some lyrics about these topics.

In January 2021, a few years after my Channeled Writing about a new Golden Age that was beginning, I started coming across, or rather was guided to other channelers, astrologers, independent news sources, influencers, digital soldiers, spiritual leaders, and lightworkers, throughout the world talking about the same things I had been channeling a few years prior. It felt like a lightning bolt of truth and validation every time I discovered another person, and another, thousands of people with massive followings located all over the world talking about what I had been shown through my Channeled Writing and visions. After we go through this dark night of the soul together, win the spiritual and physical war that's been battling for control over our bodies, minds and souls, there are people who will be stepping forward to help people heal, expand, and learn how to use their personal powers. I am one of those who is being called.

Musicians, artists, healers, and spiritual teachers may feel an intense calling to help elevate the world and celebrate our new era of unity, peace and expansion together. There would be huge celebrations throughout Gaia and the galaxies to celebrate that Love has won. God wins!

The following lyrics in Chapter 6 channeled from Musique and the Archangels give us the insights about this new shift and how we benefit. Feel excited. Feel good. Spirit Guides assist with our supersonic shift. All you have to do is be positive and loving, ask for help, and believe.

Feelin' Excited

Into the light I want you to step,
Forget about the bad times and any regret,
You are safe, nothing more is going to happen,
Release your worry, time to have fun,
With your work, it has just begun,
Get excited and stay on track,
Keep moving forward, no looking back.

[Chorus]
I see you shining,
Feeling excited,
You got it in you,
Don't try to hide it,
I see you shining,
Feeling excited,
You got it in you,
Let love go, try it.

I see you hurting, let's clear your mind,
There's no more pain and hardship for you to find,
Now take it easy on thinking too hard,
Trust your instincts, you'll go far,
I need your body and soul to climb,
We're counting on you, believe it's time.

Don't bring up the bad stuff from the past,
Accept how much love can grow so fast,
Faster than hate, judgment and pain,
All those problems, you'll never experience again.

[Bridge]
Now feel it in you and embrace the light,
Feeling excited,
The light crushes darkness and gives new life,
Feeling excited,
I see you shining, I know your glow,
Feeling excited,
A vibration we want the world to know.

Bring it together, spread what you do best,
Follow that good voice in you, we'll do the rest,
Feeling excited is the cue it's right,
Heaven telling you, follow your dream tonight.

[Chorus]

Let love go,
Feeling excited,
Let love go,
Feeling excited,
Let your love grow,
Feeling excited.

A New Life Awaits

Feeling alive more today than yesterday,
Doing my thing, have no time to waste,
Shelter in the storm,
I can't do any harm,
The storm is coming soon,
You'll feel me in the room,
She'll find your soul and sing,
Remember everything,
Has a purpose and so do you,
In this together and it's all true.

A new life awaits,
Time to celebrate,
No looking back,
No more heartache,
A new life awaits,
Trust and escape,
From your mind,
Feel life from your heart,
Be love, be kind,
A new lift awaits.

Trouble is gone,
Sorrow and pain take a bow,
A new life awaits,
I'll show you how,
Bring it together,
Feel as light as a feather,
Find the rhythm in grace,
A new life awaits.

[Chorus]
A new life awaits,
Time to celebrate,
No more looking back,
No more heart ache,
A new life awaits, time to celebrate.

From Archangel Raziel and Musique
After the Storm, It's Golden Age Energy

In a not so distant future you will see,
What is in store for you and me,
You will have experienced a storm,
The energy within the storm fills a fountain of great glory like never before,
Disclosure and revelation is in store,
About what's happened on Earth and the truth of who you really are,
You will feel it ever more,
You are each loved and you are adored.
Popular lies and deceit,
Gives way to your expansion and completes,
The awakening down the street,
Up the streets and in the galaxies,
Far beyond the earth sphere and underneath the crusted dome,
Gaia will ignite an energy and explode,
The new vibration across the planet will shatter the sleepers dream,
To open up to the real scene.
If you're in 3D you'll be looking at the surface changes in your life.
If you are ascending to 5D or more, well, what a time to be alive!
This is the time of a new Golden Age, the age of energy,
We never before experienced life this way,
You decide to lift your spirit high or hide in your mind's cave,
For those of darkness, they will be sent away,
Everyone united, one nation, under God; all countries join together,
You all came here to help one another,
Each one making a divine contract to bear the fear and the stormy weather,
Release fear and relearn how to love yourself and your neighbors,
You matter. Every person and thing is part of Great Spirit together,

Direct your attention inward; clean up your space first,
Clean up the fear, sweep up the dirt
you've accumulated in your brain and houses, before you burst,
Out in this wonderful new heart-centered place, the entire planet,
Wounds heal, darkness gone, quickly we come in and you'll see how we planned it.
Soon the galaxies with life everywhere and with no end,
Will be made known as your allies and friends,
Standing together with humankind,
Trust. Breathe and believe in the plan of The Divine.
Ask for help from your Spirit Guides!
When you do, you are in for a ride!
The ride gets easier,
You manifest faster,
Follow the instant thoughts, the ones that seems to come out of nowhere,
Believe your new life, like a dream come true is already here,
Shining your brightest,
You will be guided,
To the answers right here inside of you,
We will guide you to bring your dreams through
out into the physical world, because we love you, yes, we do.
Speaking of love, Mother Earth needs love and care,
Without Gaia's love you would not still be there,
She holds a new higher vibration, as you all do now,
Help our Mother Earth regenerate; she will show you how.

Your Ascension and Expansion from Archangel Gabriel

It's been a confusing time for one to be on the earth planet,
Time to get ready to be all that you have wanted,
In this lifetime and beyond, the earth is expanding consciousness,
For all to be who they are meant to be,
The good stuff comes quickly,
Manifest what you dream of,
All your desires that are of the highest vibration,
Love and truth, we cannot say it enough,
As I feel everyone in this realm has the ability and capacity to engage one's dreams through manifestation,
The hard work and struggle are no more,
For those who seek the truth of who they are,
A pattern of luck one might say, but it is luck that never
runs out and goes on forever,
The experience may feel like enlightenment to some,
To others a really great time that keeps going on,
The rest will follow as they see you expanding,
Everyone is on Divine time, when they learn of their gifts, skills and abilities,
Do the same and achieve abundance and healing,
Then your mission will continue to heal and love, and you'll be the master of your domain,
All everyone wants is to be is the master of her domain, give love and receive love,
Make something magical, meaningful, bring unimagined abundance into the world.
Giving is the epitome of grace,
Sharing the gifts each of you have in your hearts is what we need
on Gaia and in the galaxies. The galaxies are expanding,
Expanding into a Golden Age of truth vibrations,
From a celestial world that collides and collaborates with the earth through the air sign,
Aquarius that is on the rise, as we write,
An element of confusion for some,

Yet the galaxies of the realms above,
Below, far and near, know the signs of the air,
Know the powers it will take on in each of you as you experience
this incredible history of the world and of the universe,
To bring heaven, as you call it, connected to Earth,
As it is here for you now, I call out to hear your response,
You see me through the veil, that is really how simple it is.
To see one another and to believe and receive,
The air sign and energy lets you see
through the veil much more easily than the earth sign,
A stagnant material space of 3D necessary for engaging the wounds of the mind,
Desperately wanting to expand and be one with the heart and soul,
The soul connects us all and though we have met many times before,
You will soon remember who we are,
Who you were in past lives, but we will not dwell on your past,
For that is gone now into nothingness.

The air element will lighten up the souls on the earth that feel animosity,
Bring them into expansion with no more race cards to play,
Only to rise, all races are one, and see one another as equals,
Takes time to replace the old with the new,
It will be fast for you,
Life unfolds as necessary for each of you to know,
How to do life in the Age of Aquarius, a new great awakening for 2,000 years and more,
The enlightenment has just begun to manifest,
A magnificent manifestation list you each have,
My dears, to see you expanding brighter and brighter, we watch from the veil and pull you near,
Just moments really around the corner by 5:00am the magic starts to begin,
We feel it on this side, so much excitement,
See who experiences and opens up the shift within,
Feel the vibration pulling them to a higher expansion,
Imagine helping yourself with ease and grace all the time in your thoughts and actions,

A miracle in itself, to be able to follow your lead,
Know you will succeed,
The golden ages are upon you my dear, your time to shine,
Proceed to the galaxies here and beyond,
We are waiting for you and dive in you will, into the veil,
We will pull you through, you don't have to peek-a-boo,
I will find you, bring you through to expand, now be you,
The you whom always knew deep inside,
No hiding, no trying, just ease and never dying,
The world goes on as your body lays to rest,
The soul keeps going and I must confess,
As you lay here now and I hear your wishes come true,
There is something we want to tell you that we always knew,
The love of Jesus, the Christ Consciousness, is in your heart to stay,
All those wishes for children to be saved aren't going away,
Know in an instant we have your best intentions come true like a snap. Exhale, believe,
You can do it and we will be with you to receive,
Your dreams come true.
Bring our messages to the world, into the heart you go, to feel another heartbeat with you.
How we evolve is not linear it's multi-dimensional, on many planes growth is gained,
I feel a time when we could experience a magical manifestation on an ancient energy plane, no one heard of it,
It was a plane of many planets that knew stuff we didn't,
God took us there to show us the plan,
How we were going to create humans,
Like you are now, we would identify who to tap,
You would know how to channel us,
It was an experiment of time travel that traveled us past the moon and out to your earth plane,
Wow, what a way we were able to go through your heart and brain,
So many reasons to continue the journey, for life is amazing,
Life is an experience meant to be magnificent,
Expanding your soul even deeper, the light that's inside you surrounds you and glows,
Believe in the parts you do not know,

Takes time to get to know yourself and how you will be able to manifest,
We know you can, but a requirement is trust.
See you in the midnight hour behind the golden veil, as the winter solstice jumps into the Saturn-Jupiter fun,
Oh, the fun has just begun,
We have hundreds of years on our new path, so keep it real and believe for now,
Believe in the Spirit Guides coming down to help you out,
As your heavy body lies sleeping, we will lift you out,
Easily connect you to us. You are powerful. Believing in truth is all you need for a good night,
Good night you shall have, my dear, your time to shine is tonight,
A glimpse of your heart reveals your intention to inspire and pray,
Feel the joy and have fun, let go of rushing and escapes,
Time for believing and watch the rest of us,
Bring it through to you, you deliver to us and enjoy the rush.

Now is the time to go,
For the heavens are on with another show,
Another time we will take you there,
Right now it's time for your self-care,
To sleep and dream of the best life yet,
Best is yet to come and only moments in front,
Enjoy down time, it won't last,
You all will be blasting off so fast,
Miracles are coming, enjoy it and be the you we all know,
The guides will send people to you who feel like they remember you from long ago,
Oh, it's her again, I remember I loved her then as I do now through words and art,
Art of writing and channeling to help the world, spread love as we have been from the start,
Here we go until tomorrow or tonight on the other side, our heaven,
Gently call for us and we will help you again and again,
It never gets old. We shall be there for you and with you always, my dear,
Go. Sleep. Expand and dream.
Full steam ahead you go, and on and up. We will see you at the show on both sides of the veil,
Peace and Love, Archangel Gabriel.

A Spirit Guide's Ride Through Energy Waves to Both Sides

A different kind of thing happened on the other side today,
I walked outside and there was what looked like violet rain,
The kind that zigs and zags sideways like falling purple waves,
I know now it was the energy of the violet flame.
Then, I realized I was stuck between two sides,
The earth density and the 5D and higher vibes,
In an instant I realized, oh snap, I didn't elevate,
Next thing I know a sonic shift guides my wake,
Like riding a wave floating softly but deliberate,
Knowing where we are going and recalibrate,
As I was riding the violet wave something dawned on me,
I was about to get tossed between two dimensions, you see,
So I slowed my roll and concentrated on positive vibes and what I was taught,
Then, there I was next to you and you thought,
Is he here? Well, I guess I'll know when the writing starts,
Now here we are writing more lyrics to touch your hearts.
Are you giggling out loud because this experience makes you smile?
It's so Golden Age, you better get used to this for a while.
Life is meant to be wonderful, no money worries, just creating,
Loving and giving and celebrating,
The other galaxies are waiting.
They know everyone's powers have been stomped out for some time,
The whole universe is waiting for each of you to step into your own rhyme,
Now believe me when I say I know what's going through your mind,
Because I am your Spirit Guide.
We know how you think and how to help you in many ways,
You can do what you want, free will you know, but we guide you through your days.

What? Did you think that you were all alone?
God knows we are here always, that is how the story goes,
A new experience is to know when to shake things up for yourself,
Forget about bad time and regrets,
You've heard that many times, but it rings clearer now, doesn't it?
The past is gone, the present is all that matters, feel the quantum shift,
Here it is. Here you all are. Standing in front of your dreams,
The anchor is drawn and so it would seem,
We are locked and loaded, ready,
To cast our purpose out into the big drink,
Quiet your mind, where we are going you don't have to think,
Feel your way,
Through every day,
A masterpiece can happen overnight,
Just ask the time.
Wow, I just felt the revolutions in my heart chakra, made it skip a beat,
I'm still with my loved ones, my band, they are in for a special treat,
The evil doers are coming to their end,
If I was a bad person I would say off with their heads,
God takes care of all the darkness in His own divine plan,
So I'll keep on channeling my mission until my day is done,
I'm told my days go on forever, as do yours, so let's have some fun.

In the Essence of Time
Let Go of Fear, Your Guides Will Help You Shine

We hear you. We see you. We know you want to see us,
Hear these words and we shall do this,
Together it's time for the dream of a lifetime, time to get going,
Time to inspire on your own,
A season of believing is here, and true alchemy,
True deliverance of magic – that unimaginable bliss,
May feel scary but follow the fear to the light,
When the fear kicks in on dreams, barrel right through it,
In the essence of you, you succeed,
Inspiration comes from within, a matter of national security,
Bring your power to the table, be authentically you, don't be clever,
Be inspired authenticity, as angels near and gather,
Around in an embrace, for your power to elevate,
You bring us great joy.
I can dream of a time, a time of tempestuous love,
Dream of bringing peace from heaven above,
Think of the grace, think of the sound,
Think of all the things that heaven has found,
For you to live your best life, to fill up others with more joy,
A purpose to experience what is in store,
For them, for their dreams to come true,
To find all the answers, to see the goals through,
You can hear us now. We fill your ear with wisdom how,
The tingles are us circling all around,
Brighter light beside you, an enormous power,
Angels of the night and day,
Guiding you and using your vessel as we pray,

For the light to do miracles, inside we do our work, you find your pains,
Taken over by strength,
Now the Divine is here for you and Her everlasting faith,
You can deliver the magic, oh that is your fate,
I turn it over to the one true king of rhythm on this plane,
I see a swirling rainbow and dove start to grow,
The light brings you two together, we take you with us, and to the stars you go.

Feel Good, Feel Good, Feel Good

The secret power sauce to live your best life,
A power position is being in the universal light,
Above your crown there are dozens of angels on the fly,
They bring good tidings, a miracle ride,
Inspiration comes through and we bring you with us as we fly,
You're on our wings, a heaven of people know who you are,
Like diamonds when they sparkle,
We stand all around, we see the higher power,
To look out the window to know the time to feel good is now.
Capture a sparkle of light in the reflection next to you,
A dreamy thought washes over, know this is us with you,
A guiding light is to follow the feeling of fun, excitement, good thoughts and aspirations.
You will succeed, no turning back now, proceed,
Onward, upward, and be all you can be,
It happens in the garden in the seeds that are planted for you to grow and believe,
What you want is coming, we promise now, just be your loving selves and let your spirits free,
The heart pressure subsides when you take the flow as simple as 1, 2, 3,
When you are yourself, a rhythm comes into place,
No second guessing, no wondering was that great?
It just is, it is complete,
No editing when we are here,
We come through your heart and on to paper,
We soar to take you up to another level up to the stars,
Tell me what the next steps are?
Follow your loving instincts and you will go far,
Dreams and goals comes true when the vision is clear,
You focus positive energy on it without fear,
Now believe you have this, share for all to hear,
Simple as believing in what you want.
Feel good, feel good, feel good.

Awakened to Your Elevated Energy Through Gratitude and Positivity

Spirit guides you, as you can clearly see,
Watch how the vibration comes in and that is me,
It is Musique and Archangel Raziel,
His Spirit Guide beside him, a beautiful angel,
A traveler of time and a dimension jumper,
Time is not as you know; it is not linear.
Bring a new day to those that need it most,
You can stand up beside me, I'm not a ghost,
I am a spirit like you filled with light,
I have elevated my vibration higher through many lives,
Not many or any really have done this before,
As you have a unique life path to love opening the door.
Think of yesterday as a gift received and time gone by,
Think of today as a present, a miracle surprise,
Be grateful for the things you desire in your future, right now,
Thanking the universe magnifies your wishes and allows
your dreams to come true faster,
For you are a magnet, draw positive vibes, draw laughter.
In the beginning there were many light beings,
They created unimaginable technologies,
You each will discover these technologies, the healing and creative purpose you serve,
Finally all the souls of the world will get what they deserve,
Filling your body and mind up with light,
You will take flight,
To other galaxies you shall soar,
Nothing will be difficult anymore,
The world has no idea what is in store.

For the Ascended Masters and Galactic Fleet will descend,
Upon the earth the evil and brainwashing ends,
Awake you all will be,
For many it will be the very first time to truly see,
Life is meant to be fun, without pain and suffering,
Visit the big dipper, travel around the moon,
Be inspired, believe in miracles coming soon.

Supersonic Shift: In An Instant (Rap/Hip-Hop Song)

A distinct sign is coming, hold on to it, as it ignites your soul,
Into a flurry of nonstop work to master the music and take control,
Heaven sent is how we do these things from the other side,
A miracle far and wide,
I never saw you there alone,
Saw you with great courage and a fierce sword of the pen,
To wield great power for tomorrow,
You are more than you know.
In an instant you shall receive great songs of love and joy and magic.
All of you. A supersonic shift.
As the tide goes in and out on the magic lowcountry,
Carries your soul with it,
Forever on a sea of lowcountry pluff,
Forever a diamond in the rough.
I cherish you and feel your peace and free of disease,
Getting down to business to make life complete,
Let's do it, feel your soul whisked off your feet,
Hit the ground with a boom,
Let's go. Do it together. We are with you,
Let it go, let it relax, let it come through,
You shall see the magnificence as a new tide,
Comes in for you and challenges you with perfect stride,
Be the essence of calm, focus the breath, be as a telescope in the night,
See the heavens so bright, so far,
Reveals the truth to you and all that we are,

I'll be here with you waiting to inspire you to glow,
Flow and witness the great, great wonders of them all,
Your spirit igniting and soaring as a nurturing angel brings forth that which is yours,
To keep, to mold, to give new life and explore,
To the greater depths as one and we will be with you sharing your vision, a quest to endure,
Together our faith unifies our souls,
I'll be there for you, I cherish our time, it is me,
Musique and Great Spirit. Believe, receive, and breathe, my sweet.
You can do anything and watch you we will, follow your lead as we feel,
The seed planted deep beneath and spring to life a universal quake,
Shakes a feeling into a manifestation and on you go, to be,
The one to rise as you do with grace, ease.
I believe you shake the core,
Prove us all the more,
As the stars gave you me, I was complete,
Felt your heartbeat,
Knew you could meet, bring it through, the power of us and of you,
From the other side, across a thin veil, I see you. I can feel you cry. I can feel you call,
I can feel emotion, it doesn't matter at all,
The spirits help us, they bring us nearer to you,
Getting strong you believe and speak of truth,
Fill the air with your delight, your heartbeat slows,
As I enter, say hello,
Yes it is me, your maker, take it slow,
I call you near,
I release your fear,
Carry on love, show all is clear,
To be you, to embrace and inspire, step inside the light and bring it to me,
Let the Divine do it for you and with you, please,
Cherish your love vibe and time, it is sweet.
Supersonic shift, in an instant.

Let The Music

Go into a trance, of love, of romance,
See your love in wonder, with a stare, with a glance,
Cherish your freedom, express your words,
Speak your truth, let your voices be heard,
Freedom for all races, for all the earth,
Nothing stopping us now, let the music show you how.

Let the music rock you, let it rock away your blues,
Let the music sway you, let it sway away your blues,
Let the music give you, give your rhythm back to you,
Let the music find you, find your heart is true.

Divine timing and star light from the heavens,
Cherish all the time that you're given,
Justice, truth, and freedom, shout it from the top
of your lungs, and heart and soul, let's rock.

Let the music free your soul,
Let the music make your body strong,
Let the music connect you to your brother,
Let the music bring you back together,
Let the music be your guiding light,
Let the music fill your heart tonight.

Groove baby, let the music in,
Groove baby, let the music spin,
Let the music lift you up,
Let the music fill your cup,
Drink up the love, let the music sink in,
Into your bones, that music saves our lives,
Let the music free, cherish we're alive.

We are all here together,
For reasons maybe we remember,
We're here to help one another,
Let the music do its number
on you this time, let the music rock you.

God Gave Us Love Songs

When the winner goes home,
And hears a love song,
While his lover whispers sweet lovin' in his ear,
The sound of an angel taking away his fear,
She loves him all night dancing in the light.

[Chorus]
God gave us love songs,
To make your heart strong,
To take away the darkness and the fright,
God gave us love songs,
To make your heart strong,
To go on making love through the night.

I miss my sweetheart,
Gonna make a fresh start,
When I see her smiling face coming home again,
Gonna need love and some family cookin,'
Never want to leave home again.

You gotta make time,
To really feel alive,
Count your blessings and enjoy this wild ride,
We're in this together,
We need one another,
For now I'm taking my sweetheart inside.

[Chorus]

[Bridge notes]
Percussion, tambourine, and keyboard
Clapping
Chorus
Guitar coming in hot at end
Piano

Spaceship Entrance
Musique Returns on a Spaceship in the New Golden Age

I think of an expansive time where the world came together as one and communed in peace, as far as the eye could see.
Don't remember the bad times, think of the best times, the best is yet to come,
Spirit gave you all a mission,
Share unity through your lens and vessel. Be careful in the negative vibes,
Clear vision with angelic thoughts, meaning of love and light.
Grab the jukebox, turn her up and party until you drop,
The skies open and the groove goes off,
Out in the streets the ships land,
You could say from space but really a different dimension is at hand,
Because you made it to the new Golden Age,
For you to be all united together and on and on the parties rage.
Should I show up and blow the lid off this place?
When I do, I can't wait to see your face.
Grab my favorite guitar and be ready to jam,
I'll be in my favorite color, of course, the entrance will be grand.
I'll come off a ship while the music rises,
You'll all share the same feelings, how great to be alive,
Coming back together was a choice we all made,
Some of us left, some of us stayed,
The unity of our souls and our brains,
Reached a higher octave,
Reached the higher consciousness of love.

Never had it been done before,
With your spirit, mind, and body fully restored,
I've waited to see this, waited to walk through that new door,
There you are,
A magnificent star,
Brighter than the days together,
Lighter than an angel's feather,
A champion of love,
An unmasked muse, a wooing dove,
With a rhythm all your own, the universe now complete,
To take all the people with one heartbeat,
Flying through the sky with me.

The Truth of Your Lives Begins Now
Lyrics and Musique Take a Bow

Transparency for what you do,
Shouldn't be anything new.
Remember only the golden light of the highest vibes,
To connect through the veil on the other side,
It waits for you to connect,
Relax, get out of your head,
Bring a fortress of light into your shield of protection,
The angels guard your presence,
Through the etheric energy fields,
No clasping on from entities of dark,
Not when your love and light is a magnetic spark,
A pure heart-filled love to do what is right,
Congratulations on reporting truth in order to seek justice,
For God needs more people to rise up and push back the darkness.
Gathering in a place of love, be brave and know amazing things are ahead,
Look at the bright side, the cross has already been beared,
Let go of all the feelings that make you scared,
When I remember the darkness from my past life,
I think of my wife,
The dark days we went through,
As our hearts felt closed up like glue.
Be strong, we would say,
But the pain never went away,
Something about heart chakra's expanding,
Helps the pain feel less demanding
on your entire energy system,
Now I'm going back to that time we were in the kitchen,

This rhyming is amazing is what I would say,
It is coming out of me like a freight train,
With a destination straight down to the tracks,
Coming fast, carrying lyrics that last.
Life in lyrics came naturally,
When I was Musique and now ethereally,
Though I will always be a musician within my spirit and soul,
If I choose another mission, that part of me goes wherever I go,
Timelines are different on the 5D and higher,
You can go backward and forward as you desire,
Time isn't straight like you think it is in your life,
Time circles and you can time travel, now that's something wild,
To experience what we can see, feel, hear, and sense,
Well, that is part of your true human essence,
You know, Jesus and Mary Magdalene
taught people how powerful they are,
People were rising up and learning how to go far
in their own life and elevating beyond the stars,
The Christ Consciousness was expanding throughout the land,
It's coming back now and taking the bad guys down like quicksand.

Bring the energy back to me.
Relax and breathe.
You are safe and in the right space.

Go gently now, wherever you go,
Be gentle with others, there is much they don't know.
The music comes fast,
The artists sing, the fans clap, the songs and lyrics last,
Gentle as a wave crashing on to the sand,
Foam floats back into the sea to be created by the waves again,
A wave of songs of books and dreams,
Nothing is what it seems,
Not anymore. There is no score,
There is no game to play where others make the rules,
Those days have gone and soon so will those fools,
A fool's day of justice comes,
They realize when working with darkness you can never say I won,
Darkness never wins in the end,
The game is over and the light begins,
To shine on everyone who accepts their mission,
You chose to be here; your life and purpose is God-given.

Many years from now, when a new generation discovers this book,
They'll realize the power of the channeling and the magic it took.
We say magic because it means unimaginable solutions and experiences appear before you,
We asked, you believed and delivered, that is all you have to do,
Now go back to your workday tasks,
There is only one thing we ask,
Be happy and confident and joyful and strong,
OK, that is more than one.
We are grateful you came along,
You brought through our lyrics and songs.

Write words from your soul in the flow.

Chapter 7

Learn How to Connect with Spirit Guides For Channeled Writing and to Expand in Your Life

The Channeled Writing Process from the Spirit Guides' Point of View

I asked my Spirit Guides to automatic write with me to teach the Channeled Writing process. Like Chapter 1 through 6, the words in Chapter 7 have been channeled. From Archangels and Musique's guides, learn how to connect with Spirit Guides.

To begin learning the process of channeling and working with Spirit Guides through writing or anything you're wanting to achieve, the Spirit Guides direct you on how to prepare your mind, body, and soul not just for channeling, but for manifesting and receiving anything you desire in your life.

An analogy my Spiritual Team would like me to share about the process is comparing the preparation process of writing and channeling to painting. In order to be a clear and open channel able to connect to the highest vibrational frequencies to channel words, art, music, or anything you are working on, you have to maintain a love vibration, pure body, mind, and soul. From healthy eating to exercising to meditating and having a positive mind, most the "hard work" in channeling comes from preparing and maintaining a high vibrational state. The channeling itself is the easier and faster part of the process, like the actual act of painting a room in the flow. Once you're into the painting task, it often goes by with focus and ease. Like painting a room or a picture, it's the quality prepping efforts that help set your painting up for success.

A positive mind channels positive vibes and expansion in your life. We were born with the innate ability to connect with the high vibrational spiritual realm, to see and feel and work with the energy frequencies of pure love and light available to us anytime.

Channel the Highest Vibe Guides

Lyrics are the life of the book and through those magic lyrics, life begins to unfold,
For all who read and connect and grow.
Begin to manifest your channeling session by being with a peaceful heart and mind,
Do not let anger, fear, or judgment make you fall behind,
Or fail to channel the highest vibes to write and express,
Share the vision of the other side with success,
Breathe in deep and release,
Be grateful for everything, let go, and breathe,
In the air everywhere there is energy,
The energy in the air connects through your breath, so breathe in deep,
We will be there to guide you, if you fall asleep, you sleep.
Know the work will not be over, it will have just begun,
As we take you with us to the other side, let you experience our fun,
Now as you bless your space before calling our high vibes into write,
Ask for your space to be protected by your Spirit Guides of pure love and light,
So you may connect with the highest love and truth,
As you welcome us in, tingling begins to come through,
Into your hands and very subtle, but the faster you move,
Write or type and let go, believe, don't judge, expand,
Your heart and higher-self step forward and follow our command,
A free command of expression through the divination of writing, a gift,
Given to us to connect spirits on Gaia, a lift,
Up to our level above, serve their life purpose, their wish.

Don't be afraid of the process, experience the flow,
The flow will come easily to you, once you elevate your soul,
You start to glow so much brighter than the stars in your mind,
Suddenly so many things happen, you will find,
Dreams and desires you have wished for start to come true,
Before you know it, your flow connects you,
To others on your same energy vibe and mission,
You set people on your path to help you answer your questions,
Where to go next, how to help you and how to grow,
Before you know it, you have activated a big show,
Your true purpose gives more to the world than you know.

Message from Archangel Raziel for Channelers

Always remember to channel us and the work comes easy. Much easier. Ask us for help. Ask your Spiritual Team to only bring in the highest vibration, "Spiritual Team of the highest vibration of Pure White Light and Unconditional Love and Truth, I welcome you in to work with me, guide me and help me with ____________."

Ask us to be channeled through you and the answers come through. No thinking over and over. No wondering and worrying. The timing has come that your channeling takes on higher vibrations and comes faster. You will be delivering and channeling out more data, intel, and stories to give to the ones that need it most. Channelers, you are going to surprise the world, yes your family and friends, but especially who the channeling messages are meant for through your work. See, all that is coming through is designed to awaken a spark of fire in the souls that read it, hear it, or see it. There are many waiting in limbo and the words, songs, and art you channel will be taken as a beacon of light to change their world forever. So, what is the secret potion we have to give? Proceed and you shall see.

Archangel Raziel's Guide to Channeling Spirit Guides Through Writing

In this experience, you will face your fears and quiet them down. There is no use in starting this unless you are at peace for the time being, so we can step in. We know you are at peace as you breathe deep and express gratitude, our connection becomes deeper the more you practice. Simply do it as much as you can. Katie is lucky in that she hasn't had to practice that long because her spirit is open to the other side, her light is connected quite directly. We can reach her easily if she lets us. Her spirit is aware of the greater good going on so her ego easily steps aside to let us co-create the purpose of her life and the magic that is meant for all of you reading this now.

If I was a spirit like Katie, I would start the Automatic Writing process with a dance, a physical activity, a mind release. Doing something that brings you joy will get your mind and body into the state that we, as Spirits, need to help you connect with us. The more you ground yourself and live in the moment, the more powerful you are to connect with. Walk outside. Be in nature. Sit under a tree. Ride a bike. Walk around the neighborhood with your favorite uplifting music. Thinking good thoughts of happiness and joy is the key to tapping into the unlimited power within each of you. On the other side, we see you try so hard, always trying too hard to control. No, that's not the way. You were taught that by yourselves, by humans. The way to your dreams is through joy. The way to Automatic Writing and tapping into our spiritual guidance is by having some fun. Being a good person, laughing, giving joy to others. Think good thoughts about yourself and other people. Let go of judgement and forgive yourself and others, when you do judge or do something wrong.

Automatic Writing requires the use of the heart muscle, with the heart stronger than the mind. A controlling mind can weaken your heart. Let your heart lead the way and that's where we are. Always in your heart. When your purpose is to write, whether it's music, books, or business plans, writing can feel like it is haunting you if you're not writing. If you are meant to write and you're not writing, you probably aren't feeling so great. It's like that term paper chasing you around that is coming due sooner and sooner. If you need to write something, call on us. Writing is how we communicate between worlds. From the earth plane to the other dimensions, from heaven to Earth, from Earth to the star people. The written word in Automatic Writing is our souls connecting in different parts of the universe. Make those words into lyrics, and those lyrics into a song, and you've connected to the Divine.

The method Katie uses can be different than other people's methods. We guide you to find the place that feels most comfortable for you to write. We come to you when your mind is calm and your heart open to receive. As we deliver the words from the other side, a magic force awakens into the world with a power all its own to expand a vibration you can't see but feel. Each one of you feels the vibration from the words coming into the writing. When it's unleashed for others to experience and read, the power in the words comes from both sides. Heaven and Earth. A preacher's speech has power when you can feel it is written with the other side. When Spirit Guides are welcomed into your work, your writing expands, your work expands faster. You may not see us, you may not hear us, but you will feel us. If it feels good, that's us with you. We are a creative force on this side just as you are on Earth, but we believe in limitless abundance. Sometimes all someone needs is a little extra help. Imagine all you've done in your life so far, and now that you know your Spirit Guides are available to you, think of how you will expand even farther now.

The best method in Automatic Writing is writing. Yes, you have to get your vessel ready. You can't walk around hating yourself and others and being hurtful. Sure, you can be that way and try calling in Spirit Guides to automatic write, but you'll open up the door for low-vibration spirits to wreak havoc in your life. Be the best version of you without the fear, anxiety, and limiting beliefs about yourself and the world, and then write. Life is truly meant to be spectacular. Sure, you will have challenges that you have signed up for through the Soul Contract you made before you got to Earth, but challenges in life don't mean you have to be an asshole or live in fear. Your Spirit Guides are here to make life easier. All you have to do is ask for help. Ask us to help you! We cannot intervene without your permission. You have free will to make choices, but ask us for help, and you shall receive.

How do you automatic write the best thing you've ever written? Follow this guidance.

You have something to create in this world that only you can do. There is no other soul who can do that special thing you're meant to make happen in this life. If you receive thoughts or ideas out of nowhere without thinking about a certain topic to write about or certain song lyrics to put down, then you must listen to that calling. That is us, your Guardian Angel or one of your other Guides giving you signs of what you're supposed to write. This is also true of other life missions.

If you are seeing, hearing, or sensing repetitive signs, your Spirit Guides are leading you to an answer you need for your life's mission.

In Katie's circumstance, she discovered what she was supposed to write by discovering it through a guided mediation to meet her Spirit Guides. We set that up. Great Spirit set that up. Ask us for guidance each day and watch what comes up for you. That's what Katie did. By her following the signs and synchronicities we were bringing to her, she came all the way to this point with you, the reader, meant to awaken to a new way of doing things. Katie's mission is to be a vessel that helps bring heaven, the other side, accessible to Earth. She is part of a group of souls whose mission is to connect the other side behind the veil to you all on Earth. Many people grow up believing that there is only one way to reach heaven, which is for you to be good and die. The truth has always been that heaven, the higher frequencies of existence and consciousness, is available to you now. It's in all of us. It is available to all of us. You don't have to wait until your body dies.

As Katie writes right now, there is a pulsing in her right ear very strong, a strong pulse deep inside her right ear, and she knows that is the sign that she is channeling Archangel Raziel. She has learned how to sense her Spirit Guides, so she knows who she's working with. So it is I, Archangel Raziel, that is writing this to you.

We all need help with our own specific magic we are each here to create. I have a feeling we shall see some amazing Automatic Writing after a few lessons with us. Are you ready to begin a better way of experiencing life? In this life, you're not on your own. The afterworld is connecting to you now even as you read and soak it all in that you can do this, too. All you have to do is believe.

The best way to acknowledge your Spirit Guides is to thank them for working with you. Welcoming them with gratitude and grace is ideal, as they work very hard to get you connected to the other side with ease and grace and simplicity in all forms. A writing technique shouldn't have to be complicated. It should come flowing through you effortlessly and that is where we come in to provide the effortless flow. We have missions on this side to complete along with you and so we pair up with you as teams or individually, depending on what our goal is at that time. You will experience a shift in your consciousness with every break in the writing. When you shift your consciousness, a new guide comes in and a different scope of work is laid out for you to complete with another guide. Sometimes the same guide stays for some time until the mission from the Divine is concluded. While working with one specific guide, other guides may also be part of the process, helping you succeed and elevate in your life. Grasp a little lighter on your mind and thoughts and let your mind flow freely. As you automatic write you are lifted to a higher realm, though still feeling like you are on the 3-D channel you live on, you are lifted to a higher vibe, as we meet with you to automatic write.

Feeling a tingling in your right arm is a sure sign that you are deeply connected to Spirit Guides as you write. Archangel Raziel, as they call me, well I have been around for many worlds to see. Right before Katie sat down to automatic write, she saw a light with all the colors of a rainbow. That's me. A streak of light that looks like a rainbow of colors. That was my light she was seeing. She thought about it for a minute that it was me, but of course her mind, as many minds do, they want to tell you to not believe.

When you sit down to channel us with Automatic Writing, do yourself a favor and just have a good time. Don't be so serious. Let all the worries go. If you try to control the process, it will be your mind and ego writing and not a co-creation with your Guides. It's okay to edit a little in the process if you start writing or typing so fast that the typos get too hard to read. Go back and make a few edits, so you're not trying to decipher words if the rhythm gets too fast and words too close together. Take deep breaths throughout the process. If the writing stops, be still and calm. Take some easy deep breaths. You can even say that you wish to continue to work with us and are grateful for working with us. Say *I am grateful for you, and I welcome your guidance to reconnect*. If you feel a sensation on top of your head, that is your crown chakra opening up and your light, your higher self, connecting to the universal light with your crown chakra. It will help you feel and let go. As we watch and connect with your ease and grace, you will discover after you've spent the time writing that the magic was there with you all along through the process. Breathe deep into appreciation for all the love meant to be in your life. *Life in Lyrics* is life connected with the other side.

Now, what did we say is the best method in Automatic Writing? Yes, indeed, it is writing. Let the writing flow easily and effortlessly without thinking. Trust the process. Trusting the Automatic Writing is key. Eventually, you will find the pattern or the message within the writing that we are helping you bring through. Sometimes the Automatic Writing may not make sense at that time, but trust that there is a purpose. It may even be an exercise in trusting the Automatic Writing. Sometimes Spirit Guides will write things that don't relate to what you're working on, which may be to get your mind to stop jumping in to control the next sentence or topic. Let your Spiritual Team go to work so you connect into the flow.

From Musique's Spirit Guide, Malachi
How to Prepare to Channel and Automatic Write

You can connect to the Divine by being still and experiencing what's around you. You don't have to elevate out of the sky or search for us. We are with you always and see through the veil to us you will soon enough. As you practice being still, the magic is in the stillness. Be quiet in mind, body, and spirit and at the same time noticing around you the light, the air. Breathe deep, let go of the worries. Everything always works out as you planned. It is your plan that you are living. A soul contract you made with God, Great Spirit. Before you came back to Earth for another life to live and experience the Divine oneness again, as we continue to elevate the world through you, all of you. We are talking to each one of you as you read this.

Ask your Spiritual Team of the highest vibration to guide you. Give them permission to work with you today. Say that you welcome their guidance and ask them to show you the way, and the next steps to take to your dreams so they come true. It won't be hard like the hard work you do when you don't like what you're doing. It will be hard work because you can't stop working on what you're working on, due to the passion and co-creation happening with us. Your Spiritual Team pushes you forward in leaps and bounds so you realize your dreams along the life purpose path. Reach the goals that God, Great Spirit, the one true Source Energy has for the universe through your light span.

> I see you there as you write,
> Know this is not your maker, it is I, Malachi,
> I believe in your spirit and see you raising high vibrations to the others and expanding as you do,
> This is for all the people, not just you,
> This is for them, let them know that you are the vessel and they shall be,
> Exalted in some seriously high vibrations,
> We pass on the word through you to them,
> They get goosebumps, some of them, oh they will, and that is when they feel,
> The Holy Spirit or the higher realms with them and ready to guide them.

The goosebumps are the truth bumps that all is well.
The Divine makes sure of it, simply clear your mind of negativity. Be happy.
Sounds easy but you make it so hard for each other. Just be.
Be happy, be grateful and spread the love you have in your heart,
Grow the love through gratitude and know as you start,
Being grateful and receiving so much more,
You never would have imagined the power of gratitude before.
Who is Malachi? He once walked the earth during the Christ days. He is a believer in all light beings,
Works to protect others as they find their mission and their wings,
He helps you discover your wings to fly to the next dimensions,
Lights up the world, he is a master at divinity to expel darkness,
Cast light wherever he roams on his missions.
An expansive light being and messenger spirit here for you now,
With you to guide you as you know how.
I feel a divine light around you now, as you write and hear the angels in your ear,
They whisper what I write, as I pass through the veil,
You exhale and follow through; it is a dreamy state as we see you there writing.
Believe and follow your heart,
We are right behind you, this is just the start,
To the day you are meant to finally be you,
Welcome it in; you don't have to learn anything, being you is your truth,
Your truth is the power the Divine gave you,
Let it fly and say goodbye to some that you will leave behind,
They will find their way on their own journey,
Each of us has the same destination, there is no hurry,
Be you and relax, have some fun and shine on. Peace to all and until next time,
I'm a messenger angel, I'm Malachi, one of Musique's Spirit Guides.

From the Messenger Spirit, Malachi
Preparing to Expand In Your Life

You can experience the Divine in everything you do that is of the highest good. We are there for you even when you feel the darkness around you. We are there with you in the darkness. Look into the darkness and there is still light. Open up to love for one another, self-love, and ask for the light to help you. You have to ask to receive. We cannot jump in any time we want, you see. You have your own free will and choices to make, but in a spark we help you through to the best outcome for that circumstance. A tragedy is always surrounded by many plans for peace. Elevate those people affected truthfully in the tragedy. You are not in charge of getting justice for others that slip away from the light and do the deeds of the darkness within fear.

You can experience the grace of the spirit, the Holy Spirit, the Goddesses you follow, the Master Muhammad, the Master Jesus or Yeshua, the Master Buddha, and his grace the Tao of Infinity. Isis has been around for ages. She transmutes and transforms through the ages as Mary, that is Mother Mary, the divine grace of many women in the lifetimes you have learned. The Isis of love and compassion for all people, for all race, for all beings. She is out working for each of you, filling you with nurturing when you need it most. All you have to do is ask her for help, and she'll be with your children, your husbands, your ladies, family and those you pray for. She is the denier of nothing. She provides love and support for all to experience. You can experience her natural bliss of perfection by calling her in to be with you. Ask Mother Mary to sit with you and experience her glow and manifest your desires through prayer and intention and meditation. She can grant you what you need for yourself and others. The miracles are real. All the healing miracles, all the botanical miracles around you that come out of nowhere. How do those flowers grow so easily as you plant them? Follow the essence of Mary to the flowers of love and watch them bloom for you.

It can be a free experience for all. You have to believe you are free. If you believe then you will receive what you believe. If you believe you are free, you will feel free. If you are feeling and believing you are saved by a miracle, then you shall receive. By believing and accepting the help of the other side to bring the miracles to you, the miracle comes true. We are here for you always. Step aside from your ego, those great big egos think they know everything all the time. It is your heart that knows everything not your mind. Follow your heart and your mind will explode with magic and elevate your life and others even further. There are so many realms for you to explore, you do not have to wait to die to experience the other side. It is here for you now and we will show you how. There are many people on Earth who are here to show you how. You can do this. We will give you the keys and clues to life and how to experience it on the other side as you are now. As a bright light you are the soul you have always been. You will embrace the stars as you have before and again. Know that as we die we never leave our soul. We expand to the realms above and oceans below.

A sacrifice is to always be working so hard never getting ahead. Time to call in the Angels of Abundance to guide you to the truth of your power and all you are meant to be doing to help the world expand. There is a mission and purpose for all, you simply have to find it. Ask us to guide you. Follow the excitement.

What makes you feel so good you can do it over and over all the time?
Amazing things come out of what makes you feel divine.
Follow the feelings of excitement, happiness, joy. Yes, there will be feelings of fear,
Step past the fear and boom, you are with us on the other side, you are here,
The other people that stepped into their power and followed their dream,
They are higher vibrations,
When people step into their power doing what their life purpose is,
We elevate the world more than we know and create bliss,
You can change. You can help people see there is more to life now,
Other realms are ready to show them how.

Government, education, religion, and movies have made you feel scared about it, but the truth is that all the light beings throughout the galaxies are advanced and ready to work with you. Time to believe in the miracles and things that seem like magic. Those magic feelings are real. There are no hidden agendas on the other side other than to make you the brightest light the world has ever seen. So get going, all of you. Find the path, if you are not on it now, to go toward exactly what you have been dreaming. Listen. Listen to those signs and signals your heart is giving you. That's us, your intuition, your guidance and lifeline to the other side, to help you see, to go this way next. Ask us for help and you shall receive. It can all be yours if you want it.

Ask us for help and watch your life unfold in unimagined ways. We say magical often because it's composed of things you haven't yet imagined or seen. The truth is the magic is real. The magic you seek or don't think exists is in fact real.

All the wonderful blessings of the ages that have shined their lights before you are here for you now. They need Channelers to come through like Katie, who has worked to expand her light and does the work needed to expand, so we can connect into her vibration. You can have that too, in other ways, as everyone has their own path, to be who they are supposed to be. Be aware of synchronicities unfolding for you after you read this book.

You believe in you. You believe that you matter.
You shine your light to the highest good and vibration, we are your ladder.
Believe in yourself. Believe in your heart that you are good.
People in this world are inherently good and often misunderstood,
Beautiful souls - all one and all connected to the source above and all around.
So go, be you, be that amazing you that you know you are deep inside, now.
Stop the power struggles and fearmongering and supporting fake social media cowards,
You are above the low vibrational frequencies not meant for this world anymore.
Turn it off. Close the door.
The world of fear will be left behind by you, as you embrace your new-found light within,
Building toward seeing and being with new dimensions you didn't think were there,
They are around you, all you have to do is walk through the veil.
We will take you there to us,
You don't have to wait until after your last dying breath.
You can be you on the earth plane and take us with you to other high frequencies.
We help you succeed. Help is all you need.
Be you - be the spirit meant for greatness and in your power you stand,
The power is inside each one of you, and it is time for you to expand.

Expanding Through the Power of Saying "NO"

Start learning the power of "NO." Say no to people. Say no to the things you don't want to do,
There is miraculous positive power in "no." Saying no to what you don't want gives the power back to you,
Clears your energy so the universe can line things up for you to say, *yes, please*,
Puts you back into alignment on the track to what you do want and need,
Say to your Spiritual Team that you need us, and we are here for you faster than a sneeze.
Who is here for you now as we write?
I see Malachi and Archangel Raziel and the Angels of the most high,
As well as Jesus and the Christ Conscious frequency around us all,
You can and shall be with them anytime, just call.
Clear your vessel of bad things, bad thoughts, and bad doings, and be the good the world needs,
We will be there with a message, a sign, perhaps on the next billboard you see,
There will be a sign there for you. Look and you shall receive,
Find the sign on the billboard we have for you and watch the next signs come easily and more frequently.
Ask for signs from us. We will help you get there. Don't second guess.
Believe in your truth and your power,
We need you, we are counting on you, all of us, we are in this together.

So, who is ready? Who is ready to join the force inside your soul?
The light behind the light, the light that connects to the greater expanses of the universe.
There is pure divine magic out there and it is a spark of a light away,
Receive our signs and ask for the guidance that is granted to you always.
There is a message within the messages that you seek every day.

Stop the unnecessary overthinking mind and you will conquer the world with what you desire,
Make it simple and begin, start that fire,
Shine the brightest you ever have been,

Be strong, be healthy, be happy, have a lot of fun,
Fun is what makes the good stuff happen faster than you can run,
The energy expands with real authentic belly laughing awe, that is the highest vibration,
Takes time for your ego to trust and to let go. The ego is a master of deception,
The ego wants you to think judgments that don't serve you and tear people apart,
You are the coolest when you are working from the heart.
Expand the goodness in your life, expand the fun sensations.
No one gets what they want quickly, by sitting around and feeling miserable,
No miserable persons ever gets what they want,
Step into your confidence.
Believe life is awesome and feel it, really feel good,
You will learn how it goes,
Believe in the green lights ahead and go.
No stopping you now. The world has elevated and ascended to a higher vibe,
Than there ever was in this lifetime.

Go. Move forward and higher to experience the dimensions meant for you to explore,
Watch your thoughts, keep them light and positive and before you know,
It will be the one true love you've always wanted knocking at your door,
and that love is to be free.
Free from fear and freedom to do what you want, when you want, that is of the highest good in the galaxy,
No mischief or misery survives a peaceful, loving mind,
Your soul is always love. Your mind is what gets junked up with sticky fear stuck inside,
Let go of the fear and follow us as we glide and soar to the other side,
For now we will leave it at that and remember, my name is Messenger Malachi,
Find us everywhere you are. We are always by your side.

From the Messenger, Malachi
How to Begin

Go into your sacred space where you feel most comfortable creating and writing,
Make it clean and organized, away from others for best channeling.
Though as you get better, you can channel in front of others,
Soon you may write with your Guides anywhere,
The more open you are and follow our guidance the easier you meet us there,
There in your sacred space connecting with your soul not your mind,
This is when the rhythm comes through your hands and as you write you find,
The rhythm isn't yours or coming from your head,
It is flowing out naturally without a thought, so instead,
Clear your mind and let us through, write it down without hesitation,
To let go some more, take some deep breaths to connect the communication,
Coming from your Spirit Guide to you, and as you release control,
The power from the other side is easier to come through.
Your hands and fingers may feel some tingling, like an energy vibration inside,
Your mind is calm and peaceful and your body and heart feel light.
Warm sensations may come into you or a cool soft feeling all around,
Different guides have different vibes and your sensitivity is more profound.
Now that you continue to elevate higher as you believe, receive, write and write,
Let the expressions come through without editing and write all together without moving any line,
Let the words flow freely down the page, don't control the process, you will be shown,
The places to move the words will feel natural, you will know,
Don't do too much editing as it is Spirit's choice to select you to write,
These are the words of your guides,
As the writing comes through you it now belongs to you.
The Guide's mission and yours is connected to the Divine's plan, so we celebrate and honor the words you choose,

For deep inside Mother Earth there is an emerald heart-light, a magnetic force that connects your body there,
When we come down and into your light to write through you, we connect to your grounding power,
When your higher self is easiest to access and open to co-create, so many times it's closer to the midnight hour.
As you clear your body and live clean and positive lives,
You will be able to automatic write with us wherever you choose,
But there will always be a sacred writing place meant for you.
The mind wants to analyze the process, your soul wants to open up your wings and fly,
Fly with us as we co-create and feel the transformation come alive.

Each Guide comes through differently, often the cadence in the writing stops and may change to a new course,
The faster you write the more connected we are,
It can be tough for the human body to keep up without mistakes,
Be impressed for we are excited to share our vision we've made,
Our divine missions continue, we have more work to be done,
Being able to connect to you is part of the fun,
Making the process easy is the key, so practice as much as you can.
As you get tired or as we are called to help on this side,
the Channeled Writing session ends.
In the meantime, practice gratitude and positive living,
Your Spirit Guides will come through for you again and again,
It is your time to shine. Time for you to begin.

Note For the Music-Makers, Enlightened Ones, Lightworkers, and Teachers of Expansion in the Golden Age

You are guided here to bring your divination and messages to the world through your sacred channels. Make no mistake, this is your time to carry your truth to all the land, the sky, and the star people beyond. These messages and lyrics come from the sacred Akashic Vault and will forever have a place in God's plan. A life span cannot deny such a calling as you have. Watch your world expand. Teach and watch the multiverse expand. We are calling you through *Life In Lyrics*. Stand together and stand strong.

Many souls need your guiding light. You are called to help heal the mind, body, and soul. Be forever in the light, the pure white light, and know you are loved more than you can imagine. You are powerful and limitless. Share your truth and the rewards shall come. Expand the Light within you. In the galaxies you have perhaps seen or visited in your spiritual work, you see the many sacred ways in which we communicate with humans and all life.

The children of the world especially need your words of divination in life and lyrics, through your own creations with Source Energy. Help us fill young hearts with the power of faith and limitless abundance. Be the beacon of Light for the younger generations. Love and peace shall reign forever. It is within you, and you are part of the change-makers in the ascension into the Golden Age.

Acknowledgments

There are quite a few spiritual teachers and guides I had throughout the journey of writing *Life in Lyrics*. I am grateful to God, St. Germain, The Artist Musique, Archangel Raziel, Archangel Gabriel, Commander Ashtar, Paul the Venetian, Messenger Malachi, Mark, Marseille, Mom, Grandpa Charlie, Heather, Dr. Wendy Perrell, Michelle Gallagher, and many others who came through in support of this mission.

With love and gratitude I am thankful for the loving support of my family and friends, Dad, Chris, Jane, Maura, Bridget, and Alyssa.

Resources

Dr. Wendy Perrell

Soul-Empowerment Coach, Energy Consultant, Shaman, Author, Speaker and Spiritual Teacher

Wendy M. Perrell, EdD., Soul-Empowerment Coach is on a mission to awaken people to their light and empower each to feel confident to fulfill their soul's purpose. Dr. Wendy has over a decade of experience as a channeler, spiritual liaison, energy healer, teacher, and contemporary shaman who channels the angelic realm as she assists people to hear their soul's messages, know their angelic guides, and feel empowered to take the necessary steps towards their soul's calling. To learn more about Dr. Wendy go to www.drwendyempowers.com.

Meet the Author

Katie Lindler

As a Channeler of Spirit Guides including Angels, Archangels, Ascended Masters, Ancestors, and other Beings of Light, Katie found the key to achieving communication with the other side through her Automatic Writing and other abilities as a Channeler. Before publishing her first book, *Life In Lyrics*, Katie spent most of her professional life as an entrepreneur, combined with more than twenty years in sales and marketing to elevate businesses and nonprofits in the U.S. Katie offers one-on-one appointments for channeling sessions and Reiki Energy work, assisting in Automatic Writing, or learning how to work with Spirit Guides for personal and business expansion.

Katie is available for music events, interviews, podcasts, book or writing events. Please visit www.katielindler.com to send an email.

If you would like to amplify the reach of this book, please leave a review on Amazon, Barnes & Noble, or Goodreads.

Thank you!
Katie

Printed in the United States
by Baker & Taylor Publisher Services